WHO FEELS IT KNOWS

POWER

OF

RESOLUTION

E. A. LAWRENCE

authorHOUSE®

AuthorHouse™
1663 Liberty Drive
Bloomington, IN 47403
www.authorhouse.com
Phone: 833-262-8899

Published by AuthorHouse 07/30/2020

ISBN: 978-1-7283-6783-5 (sc)
ISBN: 978-1-7283-6784-2 (e)

Library of Congress Control Number: 2020913174

Print information available on the last page.

CONTENTS

PREFACE

Wind is created by air molecules moving en masse from one place to another due to changes in air pressure-same as everyone's life on earth is moved with desire, goals and wants. No one wants to leave the universe unnoticed. This zeal of leaving a mark behind becomes the wheel force that directs the thoughts and actions of mankind. To leave a legacy, something he or she will be remembered for. And that is the purpose why you were created. To improve and develop the world better than you met it.

In assessing the true path in which this task will be accomplished pushed man into the maze of thoughts, including the countless betrayers, deceit and embarrassment that rains on his head on a daily basis. All these have led a lot of people into giving up the task of becoming who they dreamed to be, and in search to bring back this lost hope, Power of Resolution was conceived. For you to see and believe that as long as you are still breathing in the land of the living irrespective of any disappoint or any unpleasant situation you think is hugging you today, that you can still turn out great tomorrow. Is a prophetic message full of reality-but not without rules.

Unfortunately, many are still struggling to leave the world of indecisiveness. This book is a tool you need to leave that cage of indecisiveness to control your destiny and once you do, you will see the mighty power that dwells in you through your action. That indecisive trait in you that have been holding you down for long without you noticing it is exactly the reason why I was inspired, motivated and directed by the spirit of GOD, the source of the universe to bring this piece of information to you.

It has been, tested, and trusted with full confirmation that believing totally with a decisive spirit to pledge your loyalty to your Maker, for from Him, and through Him and to Him are all things exist including you.

Being the source of the universe, HE alone will lead you to your destination in life. You are assured of breaking the chain of lack and want which often times brings you unwanted embarrassment, reproach, disgrace and insult from people around and within, which by right are not supposed to be. Because the source of the universe didn't create us to suffer, humiliated or to be roaming aimlessly on earth. You are created for a purpose.

So you being on this page is not by coincidence, rather it is a divine arrangement in connection with Supreme power, including the force behind your quest for total transformation. All these are what leads you to discover this information tool on your hand for you to fix your problems yourself. Because no one can fix it better than you wanted it. Power of resolution is not just a book, neither is it get rich quick book, no, but a tool that changes life from bitter to better. Is a book that motivate, strategize, and eliminate fear, proffer technics and lain down procedures on how you will attract your own success from all walks of life.

HE said, *Fear Not*. The major aim of this book is to kill the spirit of dependent in the life of some humans and cultivate the spirit of independent for us to nurture to any level that we want it to. Both in your career, family, relationships, health, finance, spiritual and physical life, etc. You will be learning the secret and the attitude of the millionaires, what they do and don't. Because HE that gave us the power to dominate, control and manage wealth in HIS world has no partiality in HIM.

Everyone is free to join the world of the rich, but the question is, how ready are you to commit soul dearly to the works that will land you there? Remember, the power of a ritual is not found in its movements but rather in the state of mind that results in its participants. Of course you know that is not every mouth that talks about being rich will make it to the end is also obvious that everyone cannot be rich, to ignite the fire of this burning desire in you, you must stand out.

You know the stage you are right now (good or bad) I just want you to know is naturally designed to refine you to fit into the next level that is connected to that your purpose on earth. That means without this current or present stage there won't be future or next. Always fix your mind in the future because at the end of every tunnel there must be a light. Life may have putting you into tunnel of darkness for years now but "fear not" for

HE that is you is greater than whatever that is standing on your way to success, very soon your light will start shining.

Don't feel that the struggles you face at this moment are undeserved, know that these are merely impermanent and temporary. Never you think that the worst has happened to you-No I don't agree with you because the only thing I know that is permanent on earth is change, in other words every other things under the sky is destined to change. I urge you don't quit the fight, continue reading to learn how to train and change your mind to attract what so ever you desire on earth.

Nothing is impossible before GOD. Many of us are walking aimlessly without purpose in life simply because they have not discovered why they are called. Some also try to copy others who have discovered theirs, but when they failed to discover theirs and focus in copying others that will amount to failure. And by so doing we will start looking for whom to blame for our failure. But don't worry the solution to your challenges is now with you.

In life there is a standard principles, rules and regulations that had been laid down by the creator for the betterment of mankind is called the order of the universe this orders and rules have been there before we came on board that is to say before you start thinking of withdrawing success from the universe you have to observe the orders. One example of these orders is the law of sowing and ripping. No doubt you have been observing one or two rules before now but the question is on what ground and for what purpose are you observing them? Are those rules in line with whom you want to become or are they on a crowd base belief?

I want you to think about you, and is only pure reasoning that will make you to take a little step ahead of where you are now, for the sake of self-development, some rules which will usher new ways of life will be introduce to you. Wealth cannot come into your bedroom you have to work for it-but working it out in your own path, that is to say staying on that lane that lead to the destination of that destiny you were born with. Unfortunately, due to many noise and confusion of this dark world you couldn't be able to identify the right path for your life for it is only when you are on your path in life you will find that true happiness, joy and greatness which you have been seeking for. You will soon discover your path and purpose in life but remember, not without a price.

The value of something is not found in its cost, but in the sacrifice it requires to obtain. The greatest achievement one can attain on earth is knowing who you are, why you are here and work hard to develop it. In struggling for success it doesn't matter how hard you work or how much you had to struggle it didn't matter, because you already know the purpose and that purpose is to find your passion. You have to make up your mind to sacrifice your energy, your time, and get ready to lose some of your friends because some of them will not understand what is happening because is not going to be you as usual.

A lots in you are going to change to attract that which you have be nursing in your heart for years now. You have come to seek for the moving power that come from knowledge, wisdom and experience to sharpen your mind's instrument so that the road to your goals will prepare you to arrive to your destination. Mind you that you are preparing for war against poverty, many before you prepared, went, fought and conquered. That is why I say to you fear not, for the knowledge, wisdom and experience acquired by the great men have made the battle field easier for you.

No one will do this for you but yourself for every one's destiny is different. Your goals, your vision and the way you wish to achieve it is totally different from how your friend or neighbor wants to achieve theirs. That is why you have to immediately fight for yourself and get what belong to you. Time waits for no one. Your time is up from sleeping, wake-up and face that fact right there before you. All you need to do is to do exactly as instructed, and I assure you winning will come knocking on your door step.

Don't allow yourself to be deceived by some folks with empty promises and deceitful words. The only promise that can help you is that promise you made to yourself to discover that power that hides inside your own resolution. Work fast and delay yourself no more. Congratulations!

E. A. Lawrence

ACKNOWLEDGEMENT

My profound gratitude first, goes straight to the source of my breath GOD, in whom I draw the inspiration of delivering this message of success to the world. I say big thanks to HIM, may HE reign forever.

My special thanks also goes to my lord, a prophet who prophecies my current status years back. And to ensure that his prophecy towards me then come to pass, he initiated me into the world of academic from mine infant. He remain my hero, grand master and my mentor, though in the eyes of human you are gone, but in me you live. Is no other than late chief Lawrence O. Eneakpolo Iche Eziafakaego, blessed memory Papa, I recognize and love you.

I did not also forget my late father Chief Godwin I. Eneh a.k.a Okpolokpo, also my late mother Lolo Caroline Eneh, is through both of you I became human and who I am today. I want to assure you as your souls continue to rest in peace that I in my capacity will make sure that, the light you people handed over to me will never quench.

I am not forgetting the current head of the family, in the person of Chief Matthias Eneakpolo aka Egojiolu, and the entire family members who have be working hard to keep the family united, especially those that through their link and support we are where we are today. Mr. and Mrs. Joe N. Eneh. May the good Lord continue to guide and bless you guys accordingly.

I also in a special way recognize my special daughter Princess Amarachi Eneh, who has been there since the inception of this book, Daddy loves you.

I also recognize my siblings E. O. Remigus, E. F. Tochukwu, and N. N. Blessing, including all my cousins, nephew and niece, you guys are amazing and very special.

I want in a special way give a big thanks to you my reader, you are one in a million, very wonderful and amazing. Without you my book is meaningless, and without my book you're still great and wonderful. So I really appreciate your endless support-and my prayer for you is that, GOD will continue to enlarge your coast as long as you continue to exist in the land of the living. Thank you so much for being there for me.

I did not forget you my friends and bosses, those who have vowed never to see me fall around in the dark, Mr. Al-Hasani Abdulkouddous a.k.a AK, Mr. Paschal U. O., Lamla, Alister, Kintu, Sunny, Emmanuel Kojo, Moe Aqeel, Nassir Mahmoud, Musa, LP Aziz, Muneeb Ahmed, Adukwu Naomi and Adiza Alhassan a.k.a mother of faith.

In case your name is omitted, please don't pick offence, forgive me is never intentional-because you people of good will with sincere heart and wishes are numerous in number, but your support and effort in making this book a success is highly recognized I really appreciate you all. As you saw me through the preparation of this book, my prayer for you is that, the Lord Almighty will continue to see you through in all your endeavor and you will never lack through Christ our Lord Amen. GOD bless you.

INTRODUCTION

Power of Resolution is a book designed to improve your strength to supersede all weaknesses in your body turn them into greatness, to be able to match with your dreams and goals for immediate actualization. In the cause of this, I will reveal to you and proffer solutions on how you can control or turn that your weaknesses into a living sacrifice which you have to offer as a price for the sake of that successful path which you have be wanting to embark on. In the course of reading this book, you will find out the reason why it seems as if that dream of yours is not achievable.

Dreams become impossible only when the dreamers discard them from their mind and stop working towards them. Everything in life has a price and if you are ready to pay the price you can buy or achieve whatever that you want that I can assure you. You will also find out why you have not been making progress in achieving your dream goals-instead you keep having the same result as a result of the same thing that you kept on doing. For you to see a different result, a different routine must come in, that way you will attract different result from the usual.

If problem shared is half solved, then I believe strongly that problem viewed is completely dissolved. This book will set you on another level of self-challenge to face your fears and assist you in achieving your dream goals. No doubt very soon you will discover why millions of people call Power of Resolution, an "eye opener". But, you can only feel and experience it if only you pull yourself-out to be a partaker not just a reader and observer. Then you can see yourself doing things you never expect you can do or believe you could ever do without the help of someone. The book had led and still leading many to their path in life be one of those people.

There is no active participants and readers of this book that have remain the same or still remain in the kingdom of where they were before buying it. They are all winners-except that one who has chosen to be a casual reader, or to observe the book or mistake the book for entertainment magazine. No one wishes himself failure and that is the reason why you need to run away from this evil trap of failure through commitment to become the master of your own destiny. Let me quickly remind you that, for you to be successful in anything that you do in life, you must be willing to sacrifice everything you have got, knowing fully well is temporary. Your spirit and the effort you are investing in it matters a lot.

Power of Resolution is uniquely designed for serious mined persons who has been struggling to bring out the best in them but has not been able to do that, due to unforeseen forces of oppression, lack of knowledge and information, also lack the procedure on how to apply that hidden power that lies in them for the exploration of their potentials. All you need to do is to relax and willingly submit yourself to roll on as the information in the book unfold in your favor.

Set your mind on the purpose why you buy this book. How? Ask yourself series of question like, why am I reading this book? What is it that I want from it? Because the answer you give your-self will go a long way in coordinating your mind and thinking faculty to distinguish you from being a casual reader or just an observer of the book. The questions will also prepare your mind and body to read with aim, purpose, make a strong decision with determination and focus. For you to value this book and reap the benefit you must read with aim, purpose, decision, determination and focus. If not you will end up entertaining yourself and that is not my aim of introducing the book to you.

The primary aim of introducing this book to you is for you to start shining your star and to increase the already made brightness deposited in you right from the day you were born to this world. You have to prepare yourself to grab what the universe has prepared for you right from the day you were born to this earth. And in other for you to receive you must open your arms wildly. Can you close your arms in the process of receiving? No. The key to unlock your potential is right in front of you.

It is also very important to note some factors that are there to pull you down. You must get ready to encounter obstacles and challenges for all these will be set on your way to test your determination towards your quest to success. Let your courage and bravery speak and proof your readiness when the time for trials comes. When this time comes, make sure you fix your eyes on your prospective goals-spend every waking hour in pursuit of it and every minute between in search of the knowledge you will need when you finally reach them.

The path of every person's life is hidden, the rich are not born with no knowledge of their wealth, as are the poor and their poverty. We all started with zero account number, but as time goes by situations, challenges and resolution power brought demarcation between the poor and the rich as we can stated today. Always have this in mind as you move on in life, wherever you are-and however dark the road may seem to be, know that the knowledge you have stored throughout life will be your lantern for the path ahead.

Light is very essential, vital and important in every areas of your life including the people around you. Human life is worthless and useless without light of success. Even the Holy book made it clear in the book of proverb 14:20 a poor person will be disliked even by his neighbors. Without this light the entire world is in perpetual darkness. Anyone who seek for the light will find it. As you are reading beware of the spirit of distraction if you allow it to distract you, then you should get ready for destruction from failure.

Arresting your distraction is the first step, in fact is a paramount in reading this book. If you must get value of your energy invested and also help others around you to grow then you must focus, then people are going to see the light in you and follow you. After the first step, the second step is following the instructions outlined for you, because your effort and maximum correction with the teachings are all you need. Open your eyes, ears because the wisdom, knowledge and the information have started flowing. Listing out your goals, and plans on how to attain to them is what you have to insect in your mind what you have to give in return as a service to humanity.

You need to know what you want to do with money before thinking on how it will come you can't be commanding money to come your way without having goals or projects that made you crave for such wealth. Money is not a project neither is it a goal, but a tool that makes what we are thinking come to reality. I hear some people say at times that they cannot do anything without money I use to agree with that school of thought but, my countless research about wealthy people on earth has made me to understand that money is just a tool, which comes after (not before) dreams, vision and goals-which is mental work and that work is what will invite tools for accomplishment of the work of the mind.

Most of the people that are been recorded worldwide as self-made millionaires and billionaires none of then started this journey to greatness with bag of money, but with bag of vision, dreams, goals and passion towards their expectation. Don't forget is only a coordinated plan and focus will prevent failure and it will fuel the spirit of greatness in you. Don't let the modern spirit of materialism and selfishness affect your reasoning. Money can't buy you happiness. Happiness comes within you and it grows when you are living a life you have called for.

We must all focus on reminders that we are not alone, that we are part of something bigger than ourselves, that there is a greater good to which we all owe a duty, above and beyond our own selfish concerns and desires. So you need to set your goals, plans and strategies before money, for if you allow the spirit of money first, you will end up achieving nothing. Because money is not a goal, career, skill nor even a project. Look inwardly what is that you like or feel good whenever you think about doing it? That is where your happiness and joy lies go for it.

CHOICE

"Life is a matter of choice, and every choice you make makes you"

John C. Maxwell

In today's world, where distinction between failure and success are up for discussion-makes some of the discussants crave for wild knowledge, wisdom, with serious determination to become successful. And only hard work will lead this seekers of wealth and fame into this new paths. That is why is very important to seek deep understanding towards this particular path you are about to embark on, and for you to remain strong and stand your ground firmly when the storm of consequences comes as a result of the choice you made-remember, you don't have to be among those that try to escape the consequences of the decisions they made-they fail to admit the fact that every decision has a consequences. A German philosopher Immanuel Kant reminds us of the difficulties of detaching from the state of being driven from the outside, by the forces of change.

For you to be successful in changing anything you wish to change in life you have to be literate enough to understand the skills and rules attached to what you want to do. The rules helps you to know the does and don't to ensure your success in the course. In any game there are always rules to guide the player, is an accepted principles or instruction that states the way things are or should be done, and tells you what you are allowed or not allowed to do. That means your success in this game depends on how knowledgeable you are to the rules of game.

It is important to understand the depth and scale of the two forces that follows decision making. One is positive and the second one is negative force, these two forces are inter connected and they are unavoidable as long as decision making is concern. For example, you are nursing to become great that is positive force forming to get shape in you to attract and embrace wealth and fame from the outside, while the Negative force most at times comes from outside laying ambush to attack the positive force of becoming great-through self-doubt, people's opinions, and criticism. But in all this, the power of choice has made you the master of your destiny.

Often times we allow the negative force that generate from self-doubt, people's opinion, and criticism to overcome the positive force in us. This is the main reason why after making some decisions on how to develop some skills, upgrade in life-you fall back, when you make plans on how to change your current status, a plan that will usher you into that dream life you have be desiring for, you see yourself doing do exact thing that keeps giving you the same result. According to Tracy "if you want to achieve something different, you have to do something different. You are not doing it because you like it, no, but because you love the reason why you are doing it.

According to Gary Ryan Blair he said every choice carries a consequences for better or worse, each choice is the unavoidable consequences of its predecessor. There are not exceptions. If you can accept that a bad choice carries the seed of its own punishment, why not accept the fact that a good choice yield desirable fruit?

You need to know that wealthy people lives their lives on rules. And those rules are what you will decide personally on your own, to inject them in your life for success to emerge or you abandon the rules and continue to live in a low class life as a pauper-the choice is all yours. According to Marcus Aurelius, he says very little is needed to make a happy life, it is all within you, in your way of thinking", and by turning inward and reflect on your way of thinking you can find some kind of grandness. For you to be totally free from depression, and become successful in this life you need to make that choice to become successful, because that is where it all start.

No one has ever made wealth without first of all conceiving it and taking a decision is to make known to internal and external organs that a new route has emerge to ensure safe delivery. We are living in an unprecedented age of options and that can make choice difficult. But you should also know that the choice you make now, will program your daily routine and control your destiny the way you had wanted it and it will give you cause to face the task ahead, because if you don't program your life, life itself will definitely and automatically do that for you-is very simple.

How will you know when life is programing your life? It is very clear that your vision, which is where you are heading to in life sets your universal road map through the goals and well-coordinated plans that will take you there. If this statement is strange to you then, you haven't make any serious choice that will completely influence your tomorrow. That means you are living on what each day brings instead of living on a course that will lead you to the glorious land. What it is that you want? This are the signs that will make you to know that life, environment and that situation is controlling you.

Sometimes you found yourself in this categories of people that always complain about everything that is happening around them, how unfair life is to them, looking for whom to blame for their own misfortune, criticizing everything, whenever you find yourself in this state of complain and blame, is a quick sign that you are not on a self-course, and bear it in mind that life is programing you. Now don't get it twisted, both the poor and the rich we all are been programmed with nature that is life. But the point I want you to understand here is very simple and that will enable you to know whether you are suffering for something or for nothing.

Because if you are suffering, passing through hell for nothing then life is programing you and is very unfortunate to say that you are not going to get anything except that your daily bread that comes with heavy load of pain. But let me remind you if Thomas Edison and his team of researchers were settled for just daily bread believe me, you and I would have been in darkness today. Let's hit the nail on the head. If you are working on a particular project you are sure and believe in, is obvious, natural and normal that you will experience some challenges in the cause of achieving the project.

Sometimes the challenges if not controlled may be very tough to extent you may be tempted to question your-believe on the project. At this juncture you're experiencing a natural phenomenon that rises from what you believe and initiating, making you to be on your universal road map to your destiny. You're not anymore in the same category or level with "He" that is experiencing different challenge and pain on top of nothing to give account of. This kind of person cannot specifically tell you this is my aim or goals in life because his life has no bearing or direction. He is just walking like a balloon. He is just existing not living.

Immediately you accept this fact, your mind will be stable and calm. For you to see that which you are looking for, you must believe in it, and you must quit complain and channel that energy into making a serious research on how to accomplish that which you believe. That is to say, believe and focus is the focal point in this game. And for you to cement this feeling from fluctuating from now, a strong decision that will make you to exit permanently from any group or persons that induce you into complaining and castigation each time you guys are together.

That is the only passport you need to inject change. But if after this revelation and you still allow yourself to be programed by your circumstance you should be ready to accept whatever life brings to your table. Some of the billionaires and self-made men and women you hear their name today was once poor and totally broke more than you think you are now. But their decision to control their destiny draws the red line between their then life of miseries and their todays fortune. And is not something you cannot do either. But the question is how ready are you?

No one chooses poverty from the beginning, but you can chose to die rich or still poor. This the point I personally gave word "choice" credit. The only good thing I found in the world of poverty is that it will make you to see how valuable choice is. That you can choose to remain poor or to become rich and become whom you really want to be. And choosing to become wealthy means that you're ready, willing to accept whatever that may come up on the way as a result of noble choice you have made. It will also make you to reprogram yourself from the moment you decide to change the direction focus. You must change to attract the change you seek for.

When I was going through the profile of some of the billionaires, it made me to understand that they have one thing in common and that thing is self-discipline. This self-discipline that made them to conquer lead them to self-timing, self-control and personal programing schedule. Because what some of us are facing now good or evil is as a result of the choice we made in the past or choice-less decision. May be you have been making a nice choice to break out from that disgusting attitude or from that chain of bondage, from suffering and pains, still you haven't gotten a positive result. Rather all you keep getting is failure, don't quit it doesn't matter how many times you fail, remember you only have to succeed ones and all the pains will become a history.

Becoming successful is step by step programming. You have to set up your to-do-list which will base on the choice you have made. Start implementing it, daily, weekly, no matter how little. Leave your ego at the door-well, ego is good but let it come last. Great folks of the past and current-to them however the essential part is that you are simultaneously moving towards a conscious revolution and giving birth to an evolution for the mensch. Whatever you want out of life is inside of and its manifestation lies in the choice you are making right now. Changing your future into fortune starts immediately you conceive it. Making research, asking questions, questions no one has asked yet or questions no one has ventured into or cared to look at before, this might be unconventional, and there will be many sceptics, even enemies will arise.

But the truth is that progress, creation, innovation do not come from within the comfort zone. I want you to understand that no one can make a better choice for you other than yourself, no one knows exactly what you want better than yourself. Everyone got a choice, but is very unfortunate that some people want their choice to become yours, by trying to make you believe and follow their own way of life, making you to bury yours. They don't care whether you feel good or bad with the choice they are making for you. That is why you need to know thy self and know exactly what you want and go for it without looking back, for the kind of choice you make today determines how happy or sad your tomorrow will be.

There are two strong components forces that are behind or influences human characters and behavior on earth. One is the search for happiness and the second one is trying to run away from sadness. Is obvious everyone seeks for happiness and freedom, but unfortunately, sometimes we found ourselves in the midst of the sadness we are running away from. Now the question is why do we get opposite of what our thoughts are? For example no one wants to be sad but sometimes we are and we always have reason to justify it and remain in the mood. And this is as a result of what we believe and stored in our mind including people's thoughts and what has happened and still happening around us.

A good number of people believe so strongly that until you achieve success or make a lot of money that we can't be happy. But that concept is very wrong and need to be abolished. You need to understand the fact that everything on earth including that which you want to achieve (success) is fragile in nature as you are. Think about it. For the fact that you are a mortal not immortal anything can go on negatively without our permission including that which we acquire. Whenever we found ourselves in a state of sadness we easily tag it to what is happening around us or to us directly.

And that automatically influence the way we respond to the situation through our speech and behavior. Making us direct or indirectly dependent on external things for the stability of our mood. Our life on earth is too shot to allow it waste in the hand of sadness. According to Marcus Aurelius he said, this charming and attractive world, 'this festival of life' is given to us. It is for us to enjoy it. So therefore it is your soul responsibility to make yourself happy and for you to achieve that you need to make that choice from within irrespective of any odd.

Remember there is some consequences attached to every decision that we make in life, same goes to emotions. The choices we make, the actions we take, and the perceptions we have are all influenced by the emotions we are experiencing at any given moment. You can choose to be good or bad, happy or sad for each one has its own repercussions. I have come to find out that some mysterious problems some of us do face is as a result of trying to control what is beyond our physical control and by doing that we ignore those ones that we can control. Making a choice and standing by it always is such an important idea that demand your physical support, because it is so easy to forget.

Since the choice you are making is interconnected and mutual interdependence of all that you do now and in the future it is very important we meditate on this choice every minute of our life, developing a way to turn our weakness to match up with this new path of life. A new path always come with a new programing that will oppose the old way of your life. Is not going to be an easy battle, but that is the war ahead. Two things are involve in a battle field, is either you lose or you win. And the only thing that will make you lose this fight of success is when you keep operating and responding to the opinions and judgement of the people over your life.

But you stand the chance of overcoming every obstacles immediately you make up your mind to ignore unnecessities and concentrate on the choice you have made that is if, you really want to be happy in life. You can't be happy under depression and operation. You need to understand the fact that this path is your path and that is your DNA, is your path and is your life.

Your name is already written on this path waiting for you to come and claim it, because nobody can be you and is either you or nobody. When you abandoned your path for another, your life become miserable. How can you excel when you leave your lane, wasting time, energy and resources in another path that is not meant for you? Until you make a choice, until you decide, until you make up your mind to walk on your path you can never be happy. You will always see yourself complaining in life. The question you need to ask yourself is will I ever stop complaining about life?

This life is like this, when you leave your duty or task unattained, without hiring a steward to handle it for you, who do you expect to do it for you or occupy the post? Days are gone when humans are been propelled for a particular task or the other for one interior motive or another. That is why you really have to decide now the kind of life that you want-you and your generations unborn to live, and get up and work to achieve that if you really want to be happy. That is your task. If you really know the value and worth of freedom, free from restricted time over many things you desire, you will understand that making a choice is not an easy one and it worth it.

When you expect it to be rosy all the way, the force of testing and trial will kick you out from the lane. But when you prepare your mind and know that freedom is not free in reality that you have to face some challenges in achieving that then you have built up your mind against anything that may be standing on your way in the course of your dreams. That is why it is very important you convince yourself to keep applying physical force with faith that everything on earth is a gift from GOD and not from anyone. Sometimes due to multiple of good things we found around us we find it difficult in selection.

Choice emerge immediately you know what you want from what you don't, where you are going from where you're not, the location of your address from wrong location. As Epictetus says, we are our choices; by making a choice you're using your reasoning ability to seek out the best, most virtuous behavior, by so doing you are living a unique life. Why? Because you are trying to bring your thoughts, actions, and motivations in line with your beliefs about what is true and good for your present and future.

I want you to know that the only tin line that separate you from where we are now and that place you want to be is your inability to make a firm decision and work towards it. When you fail to make a choice you find yourself stuck on a crowded city street full of potholes and stoplights with tailgaters behind us and erratic drivers ahead of us. To avoid this kind of scenario in life, you must convince yourself that, greatness is what you want and that you shall have. For you to separate yourself from the crowd you must take that step which no body will, except you.

The first material you need in wealth creation or that good life you have been dreaming for is not outside of you but inside your mind. But unfortunately, most people labeled it the lack of money in their pocket but the truth is that money cannot think and the duty of money is to bring to realm light that which has been going on in the mind. That means the work of the mind comes first. A weak mind will always find hundred and thousands of reasons to justify himself for not doing a thing. Though is quite obvious that everyone cannot be rich and greatness is not for everyone, it is not a cures, but a reality. And there will always be a ruler and the ruled, poor and rich in the history of mankind.

That is why I urge you, haven been wise enough to think of getting this piece of book, with your dream to be greater, with your dream to leave a legacy behind, you should guide yourself always by reminding yourself that riches are not for everyone but only for those who made up their mind with tenacity will make it. According to Roy T. Bennett, he says "Maturity is when you stop complaining and making excuses, and start making changes". And for you to make that change you have to choose to make it and discard form of self-limitation and fear of failure because you can't succeed without having the history of failure they work together for a common goal. In fact failure is the foundation of success.

The choice you make now will reveal to you whether you are on a road that is leading to where you are going in life or not. Your decision will cause you to make some necessary amendment in your life and once you set on this path beware of comparison and desperation because they will crash you up immediately. When you compare yourself with others, you are not only gradually killing your dreams but contradicting your system of thought. Don't use today to judge tomorrow, be proud of who you are, you don't have to be ashamed of your social or financial status today. Is not you that choose it but you can change it through your decision.

From the moment you start being bold of who you are you will start discovering a lot things about yourself and that can only be shown to you when you make a choice and ready to embrace your human nature as it is no matter what. Always remember that your future depends on the choice you make today. What is it that you want? What is it that you want to accomplish? Is all in you not in anyone's hands. Make a choice of your life and live it, all the celebrity and great men of history they all started by making a choice they are no better than you the only different between you and them is that they made their choice and followed their dreams got the result and that result made us to know them.

Choice changes a lot of things in our life. It challenges our circumstance and difficulties. Is a rebel to that situation and only you will lead the war no more no less. You don't have to see the whole of the stairs before taking a decision, take the first step you will see the next that is how it works. Immediately that first step is taken the tools that were made for you to explore with will start unfolding. It is not your choice to be poor or average, but is your choice to become rich or remain poor forever that is one secret power behind which most of us don't know about choice.

You don't need physical cash or anything external to make a decision, but burning desire and the zeal to decide on what you want. I want to live a happy life all my life is a choice to decide-no one want to be sad but often times you are simply because you believe and attached so firmly on external source (money, friends, family, relative, career etc.) for happiness, but immediately you choose to be happy irrespective of what comes your way I bet you, you will that is a choice and once you make a choice you have no choice. With the application of this rule you can never be sad again because why, you have decided to be happy.

One powerful thing I discovered since I made a decision and started trading on my path to success is that, I have be living above my challenges no matter how heavy they seems to appear, because when you make a choice you are left with no option than to live by it. This made one my colleagues to say that "there is no time you will not see Lawrence smiling like one who doesn't have a problem" and that is because I have decided to be happy. If you decide on anything and make it to be a law in your life no amount of challenge will ever make you to break that law, because you know what it means how disastrous things could be if you try or break it.

If you can't control yourself, that situation will keep controlling you. Is only when you control yourself you can be sure of handling the situation. No wonder, it is said that the greatest enemy of man is self. If you can control and defeat self then everything will fall under your feet. Making a choice is like taking half of your life savings to purchase something that you valued most, that is to say you might have thought of it severally before making that decision to buy it. You must have putting in mind to bear the pain of removing such amount from your account in exchange of that thing you cherish most in life.

The same thing goes when you are making a decision about your life, you must convince yourself by laying a strong and solid foundation based on the reason why you want to make that decision. And you have to understand that immediately you initiate that decision challenges will start coming to test your faith, to know if you really meant what you said, when it comes that is when the foundation you laid down will determine whether you will stand or fall back to your old pattern of life.

That is why before making a decision you need to put the following factors into consideration before arriving to a conclusion to avoid making mockery of yourself. You have to understand it clearly that this life is no one's life but yours, and you have to understand that is not everyone will understand the reason why you are taking that decision, because humans naturally have different understanding and different perspectives over everything.

Everyone is living based on he/she own understanding and based on their own path, so many won't be ok with your new way of life, but is ok, let them be. Just believe in yourself and remain focus and I assure you they will come back and ask you how did you do it. Most people you see today have allowed their life to be shaped by others, while some are living believing they don't have option to change it even though they want to, to some is too late for them to make changes, and while some believe that is how life should be.

But that is not true. Choice is the purest expression of free will, the freedom to choose allows you to shape your live exactly the way you want it. According to Anthony Robbins he says your life changes the moment you make a new congruent and committed decision. The most difficult thing in decision making is not the outcome but the fear of implementation that is fear to act, but immediately you understand the power behind the choice you want to make, and you align yourself with the consequences associated with it.

If you don't let your need to motivate your choice, then your choice will be based on societal or family expectations, peer groups, and authority. That is allowing yourself to be control by external which you will eventually regret in future to come if not now. Unless you are comfortable with that, but if you are not, am sorry you have to reframe it-and let decision born out of your heart with crave to make changes control your world then the real version of your personality will begin to unfold.

Excellence is never an accident. It is always the result of high intention with sincere effort, and intelligent execution; it represents the wise choice of many alternatives-choice, not chance, determines your destiny. Aristotle.

CHANGE

"Change will not come if we wait for some other person,
or if we wait for some other time.
We are the ones we've been waiting for. We are the
change that we seek".

Barack Obama

According to the theory of Change, change is essentially a comprehensive description and illustration of how and why a desired change is expected to happen in a particular context. It is focused in particular on mapping out or "filling in" what has been described as the "missing middle" between what a programs or change initiative does (its activities or interventions) and how these lead to desired goals being achieved. It does this by first identifying the desired long-term goals and then works back from these to identify all the conditions (outcomes) that must be in place (and how these related to one another causally) for the goals to occur.

That is to say change is the only thing that has the power and the capacity to inflict and turn that situation around for better or bitter, but at times it seems as if this change is not having any impact on us, more or less having positive effect. But the truth is that, there is no partiality when it comes to nature and the activities of the universe. Find out what you did in the past (i.e., if you have done anything new to ignite change) that didn't work out, that becomes your experience for you and give you the opportunity to get it right next time. Or what you did not do (i.e., If would have done will effect the change that will prevent the ill-luck).

How can you be thinking of moving forward at the same time you're walking in the cycle of same old thought, repeating and doing the same thing every day? That are not in any way connected to your dream or being in the line with it. What is it that you want out of life? What are you doing to attract them? Do you believe that anything you conceive in your mind can be born? Well am not going to waste much of your time because we got a lot to learn, but before we proceed remember that life is like riding a bicycle, to stay balance you must keep moving. But the intriguing question here is in which direction are your daily routine moving you to?

Behind everything in life there are two strong spiritual forces that comes first. The first one is GOD-the owner and the controller of the universe, and the second one is your will power. For in the beginning was the word, and the word was with GOD, and the word was GOD. First John chapter 1:1. Acknowledgement of this facts will propel your mind as you move forward. You cannot skip it for through words and thoughts all things were made. These two principals of life are the reason why you are still breathing now, therefore anything that will start happening to you as a result of reading this book, these two beings have to be actively involve for effective result.

Honestly, I really do not know why you decided to buy this book, but one thing I know for sure is that, no one reads power of resolution without experiencing unusual feelings. In life everyone seeks for success in their endeavors, life in abundance-but is very unfortunate that is only few that ends up paying the price to have what they are seeking for-and for you to have this book, that means you know exactly what you want and I can assure you that soon you will excuse yourself from the crowed because you do not belong there. And this powerful step of action will indicate your readiness to pay the price, following the footprints of those ahead of you in this game, picking yourself up every day and going after what you want without allowing anything to get in your way.

Being financial independent, living a happy and fulfilled life is the desire of every human being on earth. According to Aristotle "change is the only thing that is permanent and immutable in the nature of the universe". Change goes with a price and this price is the sacrifice which you have to make by accepting the principles of life, with all your heart, mind and body. This change we are talking about is in you, it has to start from you, you ought to believe the fact that, in life there is ups and down, and changing of character or attitude most especially when is targeted to suit the path that you want to go will make you experience ups and down for a while, is part of the sacrifice and is normal.

Allow yourself to be a beginner. No one starts off being excellent.

Research and experience of many who had passed through the same situation like most of us hold it that, if you are dreaming to be in a particular place you have not been before, you need to seek for the knowledge of those that are already there and follow their footprints. Some of the self-made men and women gave up some of their old characters and replace them with another to attract themselves where they are today. That is why you need to know those (characters) and make sure you apply them in your daily lives for the new life to emerge.

The word change is very common in our society today even the kids uses the word. Still is the strongest of all words when it comes to application and practice. When you want to apply change it will make you uncomfortable for the first time, this is to prove to you that what you are about to do is not common-as it seems to sound. All this is to test you to know whether you really know where you are going in life. *I will test the third that survives and will purify them as silver is purified by fire and test them as gold is tested Zechariah 13:9*. At this stage of test many falls back while some persist and continue.

Change is not something that is common as most people out there think. For if it were common many people would have done the required things attached to it to inflict the change in their lives. Change knows its associates and it respect them a lot by changing their lives as it's about to do in that area of your life you have been calling for urgent attention. You have come to be part of this changing process to turn your world around for better, of course change is the only visa you need to transfer your misfortune into fortune.

The secret of passing through the first stage of change is persistent, fix firmly in your mind the reasons behind the deportation of the old behaviors for the new ones. When this is done, the uncomfortable zone as a result of the change will not have any effect on you-for the initial uncomfortable zone that is replacing the comfortable zone that you previously had will turn to fun and best zone ever, and this process is what will give birth to what you are seeking for. That uncomfortable zone at the first stage is just temporary, its job is to get you prepared for the next stage.

You can find this series of actions in some of the machines (i.e. phones, PC and other mechanical devices) we use today, whenever you want to reprogram your phone or PC or format it for smooth functioning, it will first of all ask you if you are sure of what you want to do, it will inform you of the consequences behind the formatting process. For example, losing some Apps, messages, important documents, files and so on. Going through all this will enable the machine work according to how you want it. And if you observe, most at times in the course of this action it takes the machine minutes-in some cases hours to work internally on your command. And the only option left for you while this formatting process is going is to patiently wait for the machine to finish for better service.

This is exactly what happens to us whenever we want to change old pattern of life for the new one to take place. So I urge you to be calm this change is not something that will happen immediately, but the good news is that you can fast forward the process through your devotion, your commitment, the eager, the zeal to practice the rules of the game-which you are about to be aware of. According to Bill Gate, one of the richest men in the world today he says, "Patient is the key to success".

What really happened between us and our subconscious is that whenever we are introducing new behavior, or a new pattern of life as we have seen in the case of computer formatting process above, the fear in us or doubt will continue to rise by asking us, are you sure of what you want to do? Our physical body will become uncomfortable as a result of fear, the same way distractions and doubt will ask you, are you sure of what you want to do? That is when your desire to make change is been put to test, and at this point any decision you make is that change coming into reality in your life.

Remember, in as much as we all want to become rich or successful in life, the truth is that some people are not meant to be rich. That is why since the inception of the world billion years ago, the world has always has the record of the rich and the poor. I want you to imagine this, do you think you will wake up one day and found everyone being rich automatically? If that is not possible, then you really need to prove yourself by extracting yourself from the crowd. Because all this feelings are in you, and you being the main character of your life and the master of your thought, you should decide whether your distractions will continue to distract you or you call it a quit, send them packing out of your life by consistently speaking and convincing your mind to follow your lead. Until when this is done, doubt and fear can never be dead and buried in your life.

That is why you're a god and that makes you super human, differentiating you from ordinary machines. In the same way the machine will ask you, are you sure of what you want to do, is the same way fear, doubt and distractions that comes from the previous character will be asking if you are sure of the new life you want to embrace. Here you have to be careful because this is when fear, doubt and distractions comes in to pull you back to your normal routine of life.

At this point you have to prove to yourself that you will embrace the change with strict determination never to go back or continue with the old pattern, because your previous characters will just act straight without asking your permission, without minding whether you are initiating a new life pattern or not, it will just do their thing because is long time initiated attitude, that is why when the urge of going back to your old pattern of life style, that has nothing to offer you or contribute a thing to your dreams and goals comes up, you put a stop to it by sending a message down to your subconscious mind to be aware of the new change that has taken place, doing this persistently and consistently will usher you into the prospective life you are expecting.

You are a machine in human form created by GOD to perform a specific task on earth. The difference between you and metal machine is that you are clothed with flesh and blood including your sense of reasoning that is why your mind is the powerful tool you have and you will always work with it. And for the fact that you are still living, this tool will continue to be the only weapon you'll be working with until you get things right in your live. Because being rich is a skill that requires correct mindset and it's not for everyone. That is why you need to reset yours now.

No postponement no procrastination. Enough of killing that numerous idea, dreams and goals you are not a murderer, because for you not allowing them out you are indirectly killing them to die again and again inside of you. Thoughts are things remember, whatever you think that is happening under this planet earth is a product of thought and inspiration including

POWER OF RESOLUTION you are reading now. Wake up and free that idea of yours to work for your comfort, there is no short cut to success, is no magic. Implementation of plans brings success to your table.

Time wait for no one, that hard times in your life are what makes you unique, different and separate you from the teaming crowd. Hard time comes but not to kill us but to develop us and make us fit into that place we want to be, without the hard times you won't have seen that vision or desire to be that place that is better than where you are now. So hard times sharpens us both mentally and physically. Your eyes remained blind without that ugly situation you are facing. That is why we should be happy for hard times for it has opened our eyes to see how uncomfortable we are and made us desire for better and seek for change.

But the problem most people do face which I want you to dodge because is not fruitful is to avoid wasting too many time, energy, might and the little money that you have in thinking why must this hard time come to me like most people do, by so doing you're gradually nursing a negative, sad, and developing the feeling of anger upon yourself. At the same time raising a big dust will cover your sight from seeing the lesson the hard time is trying to teach you and this lesson is what will make you wiser in future. When you allow the present situation to cover your view, how will you see your vision and go for it?

Don't be a prey to your challenges rather let your challenges become your prey, when you see them as a prey they become afraid of you and when they become afraid of you, you become the master-by so doing you are putting confusion and anxiety beneath your feet, at the same time sending a message to the universe that you believe and know that this is not how your story is going to end. Your creator did not create you with negative force, the negative force is not in you, is left for you to nurture it or discard it immediately you notice it.

The mission of negativity is to make you sad, worry, and angry but when you turn it down, it will become confuse that shows you have mastered the situation and ready to learn for growth. And the lessons in disguise will begin to unfold for your benefit. No pain has the right to deprive you of your life success only you can. And always remember this that success is not for everyone. Because whatever happens to you after now whether the situation or circumstance get worst or better is whole depends how you receive this message how you are working on your mind. If you allow yourself to go down by mere challenge you didn't go down alone, your dreams and goals are going down with you. Think about it.

Until you learn to develop winner's mentality you will never get what you want in life. Winners mentality is cycled in shifting your mind-set, by prioritizing your focus on desire, on the idea of winning, on the goals not on people who want you to lose and get lost. I want you to understand the power that lies in "I AM", is high time you give your instinct audience and ignore what people are saying or will say about you, it is all about you not about them, it is about an invention an idea you bring to the world that matters. Money is not about buying houses, cars, companies and private planes, it's about changing the course of history. Shake your head out from that sadness and look forward, your life and the vision is most important thing here.

Challenges of life are temporary don't make it permanent yourself. They will soon go don't go before or with them. Change is the starting point of everything, you can't be doing the same thing every day and expect different result, come on is time to face reality is time to change, is time to bring that wonderful idea into action there is no perfect time anywhere in the world, the perfect time is now. Don't forget that immediate action to ideas is a powerful key to success. For you to attain the level of success you want in life you must be whole not in piece, your mind, soul, heart, and body must be together to attract the force of success.

You need to find out who you are, find out what your purposes are, in finding out this you have to be aware of mix feelings (unsure spirit) and fear, for there is no way you can function effectively with the presence of these two factors living in you, for success and progress doesn't match with them. You have to prepare yourself for change physically and mentally, you need to abandon some old behaviors and embrace the new one for success. You need to be mentally prepared and willing to go for what it takes to win, that is having a mentality that allows you to win. If your daily routines are not attracting or aligning with your future expectations why don't you quit.

You must be proud to say is over. You have to give up who you are now, for who you want to become tomorrow. I repeat, you have to give up who you are now for who you want to become. Les Brown once said, Anything worth doing is worth doing badly, anything worth doing is worth doing right as we are taught-if you know how to do it, but if you don't know how to do it, it worth doing badly until you get it right. You don't have to be great to get started but you have to get started to be great. No one wakes-up and become a king or professional, you must pass the process of learning, failing, getting corrected before becoming a master.

If you believe in "I AM" you will do anything, the power of "I AM" follows everything you do, what you speak after if you believe you are capable of achieving great things you will achieve great things, you can't just speak the words you must feel it, you must believe it, repeat them every day let it suck into your subconscious and you must do what will attract it. Let the power that follows I AM become worried about the change. Change start from when you start replacing the phrase of "I WANT" with "I AM" what you speak of yourself is what will come looking for you.

Thought are powerful, thought lead to action, action becomes habit and habit leads to law and law practice leads to result. According to Henry Ford, *Life is a series of experiences each one makes us bigger, even though sometimes it is hard to realize this. For the world was built to develop character, and we must learn that the setbacks and grieves which we endure help us in our marching onward.* Is time for you to begin the journey that countless truth seekers have traveled before you, fear not, for the answers you may find on the way will be exactly the true answer you have be waiting for, is all in your choice. Is only choice that can define who you are.

Let me tell you, everything you see happening on earth today, in our environment, to us as an individual is happening for a reason, and the reason is to prepare us for the future. Because without past there won't be present and without present there won't be future. Don't let your spirit be captured, if the spirit is captured, you are completely in mess, control yourself through what you think, read, the people you mingle with, also watch the kind of things you say about yourself-for what you say forms your world. You cannot be in one room and desire to move into the next room without applying physical effort that will lead you to the next room.

Great men all over the world have achieved greatness in different aspect of their lives but still they have one thing in common which is self-discipline, you have to conquer yourself first, change start from your mind, from your mind it will infect your character which will in turn attract your wants. A high quality of character demonstrates essential traits of steadfast honesty, integrity, patience, goodness and so on. Focus on the things you have control over, for life is a journey, and the only way to change your life for better is to accept the fact that there are many things in life that are out of your control, for example, you can control your thoughts, believe and attitudes, but everything else is to some extent out of your control, like other people's perceptions and behaviors, the economy, wealth, weather, the future and the past.

If you focus on what is beyond your control, and obsess over it, you will end up feeling helpless and unhappy for the rest of your life. Focus on what you can control, and you will feel a measure of autonomy even in chaotic situations. Sometimes you slip into devastation of the mind and depression easily because you fail to differentiate your "need" from your "want". And for you to succeed in life you need to know this and keep them separate. This can be confusing at times but not too worry I will make it clear for you-so that you can boldly see things that are really necessary in your life. Spending and attending to things according to priority and keep discarding things that are not necessary is part of the task.

This mental and physical exercise will bring you to self-examination because according to Socrates "unexamined life is not worth living". You need to ask yourself why am I here on earth. What exactly is my purpose of being here? The next question is, dose my current routine in life leading me to my destiny in life? Because after pondering over these questions, the answers you come up with will make you to hold yourself accountable on how every minute of your time will be spend in the course of pursuing your dreams and goals, that is the training and that is why you are here.

Both the rich and the poor shares equal time each day (24 hours), but we all spent it differently according to our desires, this awareness of time management will make you to be productive and conscious of the next minute yet to come. If you look at how you spend your time over the course of a day you are bound to see inefficiencies, noise, and the interruptions that have stolen away your focus and attention you ought to have given to yourself. If you must live successfully, coordinated and well organized life, all these must be controlled by who you. Are the right people in the right seats in the right bus?

Like we said earlier, time is inelastic we all have the same amount in the day including Bill Gate, Warren Buffett, Jack Ma of China and so on, consider what is feasible for the amount of effort needed for success. Any single minute you miss now can never be revers back for live. Now the challenging question is how does those great men in the world spend their time since all of us on this planet earth share the same equal time, equal night and day, what is it that made them so different from the rest? This question and many more you shall find because it is written in the book of Matthew chapter 7:7 *ask and you will receive, seek, and you will find, knock, and the door will be open.*

You will not only know how they spend their time but also know what they do, how they think because thoughts of the rich is totally different from the thought of the poor. So at this point is not only the money that separate the poor and the rich but the state of their mind-because even the poor can make money. That is why is so important you study to learn and practice what you learn from those who are already there before you. Because their life is like a map which the poor and average people uses to understand the skills and locate their own freedom, greatness, fame, and financial kingdom. You're not destined to die poor.

That is why you should know and understand that being successful in life is a process, not an event, is an investment of hard labor, mental exercise, focus, determination and total concentration in the picture you hold in mind. Success doesn't care about your level now or when you started calling, no, what it cares about is how serious, how determine you are to join the club of the rich. That is what differentiate you from the teaming crowd out there. Taking action towards that plan you have in mind is the first step.

You may be thinking where to start from? I don't have enough money, I don't have job, I don't have a support in life, am all alone, of cause you are all alone because you were born alone and that is why you will succeed alone. Is as simple as that. But it will become a strong internal energy if you fix that fact into your skull and face life as it is. Let me remind you what Bill Gate said about life, he said and I quote "life is not fair-get used to it" life won't be a smooth ride. Life will be full of rough patches and it is better to accept it rather than being dissatisfied. Listen, you were born alone because no one else could do that which you were assign to do from infancy better than you.

You were born alone because no one else could share the same vision with you. You were born alone because is only you that can design your life in the way you want it best, by bringing in that which is lacking now in your life and in your environment into realm of reality, now you see why you were born alone, that is why you need a direction from those whom there path was worse than your current situation now still they come out victoriously. You are already on the way to your abundance life, all you need is what you are already doing-learning the way and direction.

I specifically design this book to support the seekers of wealth and success like you. In accomplishing GOD'S purpose over your life. Having no money, having no job, or an inheritance shouldn't be a barrier to what GOD has called you to do I want you to understand that, the truth is that, money, job, inheritance and what have you is not a guarantee that you will become successful in life (*though it depend on how you as an individual view success, because many view success in different way with different understanding and perception we shall discuss this in our subsequent chapters*). In life you can only get result or excuse and when you allow your head to be filled with a lot of excuses the result will be full of complain as a result of the ugly situation surrounding your life, but when you react positively towards the current situation you will not believe the result because it will be so amazing.

Just make-up your mind and sincerely challenge yourself by applying and practicing daily the principles that are laid down in this tool to life you are holding. And make sure you don't confuse who you are with what you do or what you face today. Many are working today earning big money still they have not find their path on earth, so working on yourself continuously never be satisfy with yourself until you see those barriers down because is better to get prepared before getting there than to get there and get disappointed as a result of unprepared. Whatever course you decided upon, there is always someone somewhere to tell you that you are wrong.

Whatever you do you need courage. *Is better you die living a life of love and emulation than to live doing what you hate.*

COURAGE

"You have power over your mind – not outside events.
Realize this, and you will find strength."
Marcus Aurelius

Whenever we want to follow our instincts there are always difficulties arising that tempt us to believe that our critics are right. But the question is are they really right? Don't answer in a hurry, because we are gradually stepping down to the core reason why you're here. The answer to this question is yes or no, but, if the "no" lack magnificent obsession in it, is weightless, that is why the power that will fuel the energy that will physically attack your critics through your deeds to prove them wrong is not there.

I discouraged you from answering that question in a hurry because I believe the reason why you feel "still" or moving slowly sometime in life is because you think something is not right or that something is wrong somewhere. You also have this believe that one day things will get better, yes of course, after all the only thing that separate the living and the dead is hope. But in as much as we hope and believe in a better tomorrow, is necessary and important to make your yes or no to be very strong because each word holds a lot to produce in our future lives.

That is why the answer to the question above should be personal and should be answered with thoroughly and make up mind to embrace the consequences that due come after decision making. Because the answer you give yourself now will propel you either to success or fail because you are answering based on what you believe. And the only thing that will keep you standing very firm on the ground when the consequences will start coming is your level of courage to say Yes, this is what I want or No, this is what I can't tolerate.

More questions I would want you to keep in mind as you read on are these, where were you five to ten years ago? Where are you now? And where are you heading to? Answering and meditating over these questions day in day out will automatically guide you as you read this book. It will give you the inner strength and zeal to carry out the instructions that are guiding the wealthy people and observing it with strictness. The instructions lined out for you will make you get to your destination faster than you expect it. The choice still remains yours.

That is why you have to answer yourself with all sincerity with total consideration and carefulness. Because is not the movement of the clock that produces the newness of life is the movement in your mind. Are you ready for this new beginning of a new life? Is a journey that you can't predict when you will arrive. But one thing is certain, knowing the address of where are going is a sure fact that you must surely get there. What happened in the past or what is happening now in your life or what will still come your way as you are going doesn't matter, don't let that bother you.

Build up yourself, dust yourself up and move on. Is better to start this journey on a very fresh new note to enable you to reap the fruit of it in the end. Like I said earlier this book is more of practical. Applying every information you get here into your daily routine should be your priority, not just reading for reading sake. Haven said that, I believe you know that everyone you see moving around the universe today is on mission, but unfortunately, many have not discovered theirs and most of us are sometimes confuse in life and our aim and purpose as an individual differs.

For those who have discovered theirs it became a propeller that wheeled or wheeling them to their destination. For the fact that your assignment on earth and that of those criticizing you are not the same doesn't mean that your dreams are not reachable or is impossible, for there is nothing like impossibility before GOD (Luke 1:37). They are not in you to see what you have got inside and they are not GOD who revealed the vision to you. The differences in our mission in life doesn't give anyone right to criticize you, never you admit to anyone criticism.

The problem most people face at times is the inability to discover or know the purpose why they are on earth (*we shall discuss in details on how to discover your purpose in our subsequent chapters*), that is why our mind keep wandering, thinking about what the naysayers are saying whether they are right or wrong. Not being sure of what we actually want in life or where to go brings a lot of confusion in our system. But the truth is that Creator can never be an author of confusion don't make HIM look like one.

Rule number one don't allow worries to distract the state of peace in your mind. Thinking, disturbing and worrying yourself for not being where you want to be can never and never make you to be there. But thinking and planning on how to get there tomorrow will make you to be there. Find peace in knowing that the darkest moments in your life are merely prerequisites for the life of abundance you are meant to have. Your mind must be at peace before something new can come out of it. Nothing good comes out in a state of war-your mind is at war whenever you allow yourself to be battling with what is out of your control.

Things of the past, fear and worries, when you dowel in all these, you are not just wasting your time, you are also wasting the energy that you could use in transforming your life into something better. But the good news is that your fear and worries have lost their grids, by letting you to pick up this book-because, your fear will soon be exposed for you to gain your freedom and ground once again. In other for you to live a life of your dream, a life of abundance, riches, wealth and financial independent which you were created for and for you to achieve that you must have courage and free your mind.

Between where you were, where you are now, and where you are going in life is what I called the border, between limitation (lack) and unlimited (abundance) land. You are so uncomfortable with the way things are going, you are tired of staying in this border, due to lack, you want more out of life all these and more are the reason why you have been struggling, working hard to attract riches, fortunately all these are now in the past. In the course of this book you will be equipped with mental metal to face and challenge back whatever that has been or will stand on your way to success.

For the fact that you have seen where you want to go and where you don't want to be is a clear indication that you are in the middle of the rich and the poor that is the border, at this point of pain you are now, many people that are in this border will turn back and remain a failure because they are not called to be great even though they wish to, but due to their idiosyncrasy they are not willing to pay the price of persistency to continue they fall back which is easy everyone can do it. While the courageous ones like you continue to move forward because they have seen their path and willing to pay the price.

Now you are close to your destination, is no sense going back for you have come a long way. Always have this in mind as you move on in this great path of life. Wherever you find yourself in this journey, and however dark the road may seems to be know that the knowledge you have stored throughout this journey will be your lantern for the path ahead. That is why you have to pick up courage to continue moving forward. According to Henry Ford "life is a series of experiences, each one of which makes us bigger, even though sometimes it is hard to realize this. For the world was built to develop character, and we must learn that the setbacks and grieves which we endure help us in our matching onward".

The world of the rich is not the same as the world of the poor, many are in the world of the poor, but only few are there in the world of the rich, this should draw your mind close to see how enormous the task ahead is. That is why you need to pay the price of working hard to exit from that border, the different between the self-supporting books you have red in the past and the Power of Resolution is that you will see clearly the bridge that you need to cross and the ones to burn. Because if you always do what you've always do, you'll always get what you've always got says Henry Ford.

You will begin to see how powerful your self-decision making can be, because from this one decision will come 90 percent of all your happiness or misery. A lot of information will be flowing and that is mostly what you need at this pointing time. Probably you may have come across those words but nothing or little do you know how powerful they can be when strictly applied. Is time to self-challenge that is my mission here to help you cross over to the next level so that you will do the same to those looking up to you for survival. My happiness is that, you will soon discover the power that hides inside your own resolutions.

Remember, doing exactly as you have been instructed in this book is the only thing that is required of you, for the power of a ritual is not found in its movement but rather in the state of mind that results in its participants. Sometimes you found yourself very sad as a result of where you found yourself in life to the extent that you will be tempted to ask yourself what am I living for, at this state of mind you wouldn't want to discuss, talk or even share anything with anyone. Some went as far as committing suicide just because the way things are going. Don't be a victim, don't use today to judge tomorrow.

Eighty to eighty five percent of people out there if ask will tell you that the major reason for their unhappy mood all the time is because of lack of money, but I tell you money is not your problem right now, money is not a goal or a project and is not a means of personal enrichment instead, is a tool that can be used to fulfill each person's duty to the advancement of the human species. Therefore, the source of all good things including what you have, knows that you need more but HE want to see how managerial you are.

That situation you are in, right now is just a perfect one don't get me wrong, but the truth is that whenever you are facing a sever challenge your mind is normally at the sharpest stage to think outside the box, that time is passing through test that create credibility that will set you on a higher realm of that financial independent you have be dreaming for, all you need is information and tools to explore. Seek knowledge, wisdom, and experience to sharpen your mind's instrument so that the road to your goals will prepare you to your destination.

An investment in knowledge is the safest of life's gambles. You now agree with me when I say that lack of cash in your pocket is not really the problem but your inability to see things clearly. But even the lost can be led to the truth, fear not for he that follows the light can never get lost in the darkness of this world. Yes, very soon you will celebrate that situation and understand why I said is a perfect one, because that is where your success will emerge from-if only you resist the cloud of anger from pushing you into desperation.

That situation is just a wall standing between you and your success. Without it, what then will you break to become successful? That is why I urge you don't force yourself out of it rather grow through it. Be calm for without that situation you won't see the need to migrate to the next level or even value the state of the wealthy or the rich when it comes. If you cannot learn to manage your life with a little, how can you expect to manage it with a lot? You are passing through screening of life. Some people couldn't wait for the screening to be over they quit and go back (because that is the cheapest and simplest thing anyone can do) while some stayed patiently and won.

I want you to view that your situation with different perspective other than the way you have been seeing it, you will notice that the situation is just an eye opener for you to see that you can do and achieve more than that. Though you may feel that the struggles you face at this moment are undeserved, know that these are merely impermanent and temporary. Don't see that condition as a bad impart, start seeing it as a positive impart and accommodate it with positive spirit because is already in existence, while you accept the responsibility to change it.

When you embrace it in that way, you have shown that you have received the message it brought to you, which is the need for you to go, for you do not belong there. You have to understand the core message that condition is trying to share with you all this while, that ugly situation is a wall standing between you and your success, and that wall is me (says the situation) you must break me if you desire to be successful, this process is what gave birth to "Breakthrough". If you keep it aside what then will you break to get through?

Let's take a look in the case of David and Goliath in the bible, Goliath became an obstacle to David and for David to gain victory, he has to bring Goliath down what did he do, he summoned courage, he never allowed his physical appearance to intimidate him, not at all, David saw Goliath as one of those animals that used to come after his sheep's in the bush, with that view and how he used to kill them in his head, Goliath automatically became another animal victim that need to be killed for his people to live, that is courage, that spirit saw the end of Goliath till date.

So don't be scared of anything is just meant to be that way you cannot change it with your physical strength but with your believe, faith, will power, and courage you will see the end of that unwanted situation in your life. Most at times we allowed ourselves to be carried away by illusions over riches, wealth acquisition is not something you wake-up and found beside your bed. Is a process, it involves planning, it involves determination, it involves courage to move from where you are to where you never been. You want to be the captain of your life, you want to live a life of unlimited, you want to be influential in your state, community, in your environment, you want self-autonomy, and what is it that you want? Without courage am sorry, you may find it hard to get.

It takes courage to be different, you need to convince yourself that you have come a long way to quit now, and is too late to go back. I want you to know that where you are trying to go is no more far from where you are right now, and for you to retain and maintain it, it depends on how you set your ground before your arrival if not you will have yourself to blame. The universe is testing everything including your capability of handling such wealth you are dreaming to acquire. That is why you have to prove yourself and remain focus on the path and have it in mind, always, that everything will soon be over in no distant time.

Don't allow anyone to talk you out of your dream, you have to be aware of day spoilers, day provokers, dream takers, dream killers and life destroyers, they are everywhere and you cannot avoid them. Those kind of people only have success on their lips, because due to their idiosyncrasy nature they can never see the four wall of success, touch it or gain entrance. They already know this fact themselves that is why they try to bring you to their low class by all means so that all of you will be in the same category. Because as soon as you are convinced by any of these their traits, they have gotten you. So sometimes silence is the best answer to a fool.

People without vision, goal, aim or direction in life are prone to distract and disturb your inner peace of creativity- even try to instigate fear in you because they know that you are far ahead of them. Jane He Austen once said, there is a stubbornness about me that never can bear to be frightened at the will of others. My courage always resist at every attempt to intimidate me. GOD has already assured you of safety when HE said "fear not" why then do you limit yourself over fear of unknown haven't you heard that, what a man feared most is what comes to him.

How long will you continue saying "I will" "I want" don't you know that once you seen that vision in your head you can as well achieve it, and if you can conceive it, you can as well give birth to it, all you need to do is to work towards that goal start with little effort. Always remember, success is not for everyone and richness is not an event is an act and is a process. For you to be whom you want to be in life you need to have courage without courage you are going nowhere. For you to be successful in life you need courage, for you to stand out from that teeming crowd you need courage, for you to be that person you were created to be you need courage.

It is only courage that will push you to act on that vision you see inside on the outside, you need courage to ignore them that are criticizing you, they are there to fuel your fear to quit, and when you quit you automatically become a loser, you need courage to say no, you need courage to say enough is enough, failures always have associate and support, you can join them no problem but note this, for you to become somebody in life you need courage, any opinion against your goal is a mere noise. Your source in life and your goal should be your courage.

If you don't want to be somebody in life be like them, think like them, walk like them, and eat like them says TD Jakes, don't change be mediocre. Is only courage that will opt you out from that vicious cycle of failure and poverty, you need courage to take the bull by the horn. Courage is the bedrock of everything we do and still doing on this planet earth. Even in the scripture it took courage for Christ to allow HIMSELF to be kill for the sake of mankind. It took courage for all the great men and women of this world that you know and hear about to achieve tremendously all the things that you and I is enjoying today.

Talk of Thomas Edison the man who produced electric bulb after many times of failure but he did not allow his countless failures and criticisms from the observers to stop him, because he know what he saw in his vision very clearly and he didn't give-up until he accomplished it, what of Wright Brothers the first men that built aero plane that we fly today, what of Alexander Bell a man credited with inventing the first practical telephone, what of Tim Berners Lee the man who developed the http:// protocol for the internet making the World Wide Web, just to mention but a few.

Before all those men accomplished these great successes, do you think they didn't encounter challenges? Of course they do, but what opted them out from being a failure is because they were obsessed with their vision and goal-to extent that they didn't allow their challenges or opinions of others to drown what their instincts is saying over the vision they had. They listened and followed their intuitive vision with tenacity, and hard work towards the goal until it was accomplished. I hope you are following?

Because becoming great is also a skill and you need to learn before you can perform.

According to C. Joy Bell C. she said, don't be afraid of your fears, for they are not there to scare you. They are there to let you know that something is worth it. Your willingness to wrestle with your demons will cause your angels to sing, that is to say you have to make yourself available, that is the only thing your source (GOD) want from you, HE is your master and you are HIS product HE is after your success, HE loves you that is why HE like seeing people praise HIS product (you and what HE has achieved through you) because when people praise HIS product the glory returns back to HIM. For you to be courageous you need to stand firm for what you believe even when death is involve because that is your belief and that is your life.

FEAR

> Of all the liars in the world, sometimes the worst are
> our own fears.
>
> Rudyand Kipling

Don't serve as a means to an end because of fear of unknown. Many had served under this fear of what will be, many are still serving and many are unknowingly warming up to join the service. Remember many are called but view are chosen. Where did you belong to in these categories of people? Those that are serving or those that will join the service their decisions are always based on acquiesce. If you are among the last two set of people then count yourself lucky to have discovered this book, because even those that was serving as a means to an end for some group of people, organizations, individuals, relatives etc. without knowing it from ab initio, later discovered what you are about to discover right now, that made them to take that strong decision that gave them permanent freedom.

Fear was a major motive of ancient Greek epic poetry and drama, it was a topic often treaded by biographers and historians of the period and explicitly analyzed by philosophers and physicians. But due to the nature and the purpose of which this book is designed, we shall channel our focus on physiological and pathological aspects of fear as they appear in the thought of men.

Before we continue, I want you to know that in reacting to this topic "fear", each philosopher that reacted on this topic was influenced by certain broad explanatory assumptions that governed his thinking not only about fear but about universal nature-about the cosmos in general, including what the Greeks liked to call the living microcosm, man.

Let's take a sharp look at the word fear, what exactly is fear? That has been limiting millions of people from achieving their goals, limiting the progress of men. Well, let me quickly spill the odorous, putrid beans so that the snoring slumber land will be awakened by the insomnia of its truth and of its reality. Fear is a powerful and primitive human emotion. Is a natural emotion and a survival mechanism. That is to say this emotion responsible to fear is highly personalized. Because fear involves some of the same chemical reactions in our brains that positive emotions like happiness and excitement do.

Aristotle was caught up in the tradition that the complexities of the cosmos are reducible to pairs of opposites such as hot versus cold, dense versus rare, potential versus real, and the like. His predecessor, Plato, influenced by the same tradition, had made fear the opposite of hope, asserting that fear is the expectation of evil and hope the expectation of good. Aristotle also made fear the opposite of confidence and added that fear is the expectation of such evils as poverty, friendlessness, dishonor, pain, and especially death.

Man has many enemies in life, and the greatest of all enemy is himself. And until you kill the enemy within, the enemy outside will do you no harm. Don't let any single minute to pass by without sowing a seed of great fortune. Say no to fear, say no to procrastination and unnecessary distractions. Man always found himself standing in the midst of what he want to do, desire, how, criticism, fear of discrimination, fear of death, fear from being misunderstood, fear of lose, fear of humiliation, fear of being hurt, fear of pain, fear of losing your friends, fear of failure, fear of what they will say, fear of unknown and so on. Which of these fears are hunting you as you are reading now?

Chances are, you will be able to relate to at least one or more of them at some point in time. I was a victim of some of them above, these fears kept me in the cage for years, but when I discovered the great harm I was causing to myself by accommodating these fears in me I was left with no option than to break the chain. I was so ashamed of myself for haven served this feelings for years limiting myself and my potentials for progress. Yes I agree with you that life is tough, but I will tell you something now and you may not experience it until you try it. Because when you read and didn't practice you just entertained yourself.

I usually belong to the club of people that always advocate how strong and how tough things are, but here is what I noticed immediately I dusted myself up from the bondage of fear, I experienced freedom within me. I did not leave the planet for another, I wasn't transformed into immortal being (but I was internally transformed anyway), in fact I didn't get promotion from my work place, no salary increment. But what I know is that before I took that decision to leave the world of fear and now, I noticed it was just a feeling of fear I personally configured strongly into my mind.

I became free and fearless because I turned everything I was passing through then and view them as a needful sacrifice which I must pay to get to where I am today. You have to trick your mind, it works for me and it will for you because we all are human. Is very unfortunate that 70-80% of people out there are still harboring and serving this virus feeling I called fear, without even noticing the harm they are causing to themselves and to their entire generations yet unborn. Marie Curie once said that "nothing in life is to be feared. It is only to be understood." And immediately you clearly understand a thing and how it is, you will be fine and free.

You have to be truthful to yourself and face the reality of life. Stop looking into your future with fear of what will ensue. And stop looking at that situation you are today with anxiety. If you have been pursuing shadow instead of reality quit immediately. Greatness, being successful in life is not a joke, you have to wake up to some responsibilities attached to greatness. Becoming successful is a reality and serious business, and it involves a lot of mental and physical exercises to get things done. The reason why I allowed us to glance through the definitions of fear is for you to see and acknowledge the fact that fear is only a feeling and emotional reaction from inside to the outside events.

Happiness, sadness, excitement and fear are all feelings which has portion in our brain. You alone can allow and activate any feeling to turn you on at any given situation. The fear response starts in a region of the brain called the amygdala. The amygdala activates whenever we see opposite of our expectations. For example, whenever we see human face with an emotion expressing disapproval with great criticism towards our vision, goals or things that we want to accomplish or the kind of life style we want to live, this reaction is more pronounced with anger and that brings a threat stimulus, such as the sight of a predator, triggers a fear response in the amygdala which activates areas involved in preparation for motor functions involved in fight or flight.

Success is not going to allow you have access to it freely, that is why you have to fight to the end. You have to prepare yourself to combat your challenges or run away which is commonest thing in the life of the losers, running away, shying or feeling lazy to do the needful for what they want to become. In the course of life fulfilment, desires, potentials, happiness and being successful, living not just existing you must see ugly things you never see before in your whole life, you will hear things you never hear before you will be mocked without no reason. If I don't tell you this truth I am not being honest and sincere to you.

All this is for you to prepare for the journey ahead, because is not an easy one. Don't let anyone deceive you, so you won't land yourself in a state of oh! I thought is like that or simple as ABC. But you can't be a reader of this book and still be a loser that I can assure you, unless you did not make use of the message, or after reading you still can't figure out your vision and mission or you are not yet hungry to succeed. Is better I let you know the nature of the road for you to make up your mind now and face the war against failure, don't be a coward.

Success has multiple and well equipped warriors with highly sophisticated weapons in its arsenal to screen out unprepared ones. Sometimes we raise our fears with our own hands through the way we think or view some issues confronting us. Sometimes we think we can predict the outcome of the path we have chosen and when things fall apart we become dismay. See you don't dictate or command nature on the kind of trails, challenges it will give you. As you are on this road, success itself doesn't know who will finally be crowned, but he knows one thing for sure, that is not all who started it will make it to the end.

That is why you have to be tested through challenges, those challenges are warriors of success to attack you in the form of temptations, trails, challenging every step you take. Sometimes it makes you feel stranded on the way all these are to scare and test your level of determination to succeed, to push forward. But when you face all these, remember, is honorable to die in the field, in the course of pursuing your freedom than to die in your shell of fear as a coward.

I believe you are getting awake. Lying on someone's promise is a disaster. Let's look at it from this angle, humans possess the same nature with weather that simple means if weather can change unnoticed, human beings can as well change as a result of unprecedented circumstance that befalls humans here and there on earth-I hope you are reasoning. Or it might be on purpose, to keep you under their control and command. Ok imagine that all the asset of your promiser is been put for cell, can the proceeds made from the sales buy all your goals and all that you desire? No one can give you what he don't have. I want you to be hungry to succeed yourself, I want to see that tears of adversity turning into tears of joy.

According to Oxford Dictionary, Fear is unpleasant emotion caused by the threat of danger, pain, or harm. Therefor is only you that have the magical power to strike fear into those areas that are scaring you all the time. I want you to ask yourself how long will I continue being scared? How long will you continue in languishing in lack and want, why don't you take the pain once and be free forever. No pain or harm last forever, but the decision you make now will serve throughout your life time. In our subsequent chapters you will learn how to invest your energy in a fertile land of your desire for a banquet harvest.

You have to put your spiritual and physical force in a bid to put a strong front and dislodge the ruling fearful force that has been limiting you from reaching your goals all this years. And united to Learning to handle fear and overcoming it, even if that's sometimes just for ten or thirty seconds so you can take an important action, is critical to living your life fully. In a real sense fear is no external thing, rather internal. Fear arises in us when we start accommodating people's opinions or nursing in mind what they will or will not say when we do what we love doing for our own good, or what will be the consequences of the action we are about to take, fear of lose and fear of criticism.

This is what happens to us whenever we allow all these to go on in our mind, and give deaf ear to what our instinct is saying about us-immediately we start paying attention to every opinion that passes by concerning our dreams and what we want to do-we start creating unimaginable distance between us and our dreams, by so doing we start depressing and disorganizing our system. And that brings us into the state of confusion, at the same time making us lose our sense of reasoning, concentration and focus. If all these things happens to us what then is left of us?

Of course when all these took place in you, you are no more happy by then if care is not taken you will start developing a habitual angry, upset at everything life brings, at the same time making you unable to see opportunity in any situation regardless of its presence. You will not be happy with your job, the environment, everything becomes irritating to you, simply because you allowed people to disorganize your whole system with their own opinions. Immediately you find yourself in this kind of situation you lose your base and sense of humor. At this point nothing differentiate you from ordinary balloon that is floating around without direction.

But sometime even the balloon can be arrested by the owner and place it somewhere. Get your fears arrested or your fear will keep shrinking your intuitive voice from coming out and when that happens you are permanently stuck-up. All these are mere distractions and you have to be very careful. Sometimes our fear come from when we start thinking "HOW", how is all these dreams of mine going to happen, at the same time we forget that if, Thomas Edison were thinking of how we wouldn't have known what is electric bulb today, have you thought of that? Same goes to other great achievers. No one were born with innovation but everyone can innovate including you.

You have to understand that the ways of GOD are not the ways of man, another source of our fear is that some of us have lost focus and shifted from the original setting-set by our source of breath from the infant to achieve greatness, and haven lost focus and shifted from the original setting we automatically lost the purpose of our existence, that is why fear is everywhere around us, because no one was created without a gift. Because of this shifting from the base, we now find it difficult to reconnect back, that is why we found our self-asking how will all these happen?

And the very moment you start asking yourself how will all this going to happen, the next thing you see is fear, it jumps in immediately it will make you to judge your dreams with your current status, before you know what is happening you're already doubting the possibility of that dreams coming to pass. Including the external voices telling you is not possible, no one has done it before, what makes you think you can do it, stop and stuffs like that. Listen, nothing is impossible under the surface of the earth, the scripture made it clear that, there's nothing impossible for GOD to do. It's not your business to know "How" your role is just to follow with total submission to GOD's command and have faith, believe in yourself nothing more. That is your own path then leave the "How" for the master to handle that is HIS job HE knows how to do it best.

You don't follow the Great of the greatest with carnal eyes, we follow HIM sheepishly-believing HE knows it all-while we keep our mind on information's that we are getting, working on it, focusing on the future not the present, and taking control of things under us today. Here's a little scenario to illustrate my point, you remember the case of Abraham and his son Isaac, after many years of Abraham's childlessness, GOD finally gave him a son, after a while the same GOD ask him to sacrifice the same son as a living sacrifice to HIM, now if wasn't the fact that Abraham was following GOD sheepishly, he would have refused the order, Abraham's faith was tested and confirmed worthy of his blessings, immediately GOD provided him a giant ram for the sacrifice.

In the course of greatness it is of great important you force your eyes closed to some things you see or will see on the road that is not pleasing. Warren Buffett one of the richest men in the world today started his journey to greatness by purchasing a six-pack of coke for 25 cents and sold each can for a nickel. History also hold it that he also sold magazines and gums from door to door. What are you afraid of? What are your limitations? What is holding you down? you have already been taught on the previous chapter, change is a process, it is also important for you to know the difference between knowing and acting. For you to remain in the home of change and rep the fruit of it you need to be courageous not fearful. According to Thucydides he said, and I quote "the secret of happiness is freedom and the secret of freedom is courage" end of quote.

You need to be brave and bold, is an indication that prove the fact that you know what you are doing and where you are going. Because braveness and boldness are not for the weak or double minded person. Before you become successful in life you have to be strong and acknowledge the fact that you are on this mission alone. Courage involves deliberate choice in the face of painful or fearful circumstances for the sake of worthy goal. Your time is limited, so don't waste it living in fear or in someone else's life. Don't be trapped by dogma which is living with the results of other people's thinking.

Your circumstances does not make you rather it reveals whom you are, don't let the noise of people's opinions drown out your own inner voice. You need to bring out that beast in you to attack back those things that has been obstructing you from following your heart and intuition. See, mountain can only be mountain and stone can only be stone. Human beings have every potential in them to transform themselves to be and become whatever they want in life through the power of reasoning that is why humans are different from animal and things.

If you really belief in your name, in your vision and dreams, with burning desire elevate them, then you have to stand firm on ground with your face faced up and straight, stop looking sideways. History is made by those who take risks, who stood on principle, who defy expectations and conventional wisdom. The battles are won by those who are willing to go further, to go alone, to do it a way it's never been done before. For standing firm by it irrespective of what comes out of it is what makes you who you are.

Martin Cooper, American engineer Born in the year 1928 once says your vision determine your mission, your mission determine your action, your action determines your character and your character expose you to the people out there that you have made a choice and that choice is who you are. And from the moment you make a choice you decide what and when things will start happening in your life. That will make you to influence and control your world including your happiness, joy, time, and being a very free person.

I want you to know that whatever experience you will experience after reading this book, depend on how you handle or make use of the contents on it. You may finish this book becoming the person you want to be, breaking the chain of poverty turning your life around positively for that is the purpose of introducing the book to you, at the same time I want you to be aware of the dangerous smooth slippery ground that awaits you, procrastination, yes procrastination, the truth is that everyone wants to be rich, but is very unfortunate, that can't be possible. Of course not, for royalty is not for everyone, same goes to success. That is why is only for the brave, bold and courageous ones will scale true.

You have to do what you think is right. For you, for your family, for your country, for what you belief in, the rest doesn't matter. Marcus

Aurelius was a Roman emperor from 161 to 180 A.D., He was trained in Stoic philosophy, and one of his Stoic practice was to stop almost every night to practice a series of spiritual exercises-reminders designed to make him humble, patient, empathetic, generous, and strong in the face of whatever he was dealing with. History hold it that despite Marcus Aurelius' privileges as an Emperor, he had a difficult life.

The Roman historian Cassius Dio mused that Marcus "did not meet with the good fortune that he deserved, for he was not strong in body and was involved in a multitude of troubles throughout practically his entire reign." But throughout these struggles he never gave up. I want you to count yourself as one of those that are already at the top of success, by promising yourself with all sincerity that you will not give up, that you are ready and willing to do all the needful and carry out all the exercises mental and physical outlined for me on this book to be successful. And so shall it be unto you because whatever a man think he become.

Have you ever ask yourself why is it that everyone talks about being rich but only few end up making it. Is success selective or partial? The answer is no, and not that those who didn't make it are disable, not that they are blind, not that GOD hate them either, no far from it, the answer is very simple, they lack the mental and physical strength, and focus to develop themselves to become who they want to be. Henry Ford didn't make any mistake when he says that thinking is the hardest work, which is probably the reason so few engage in it. Some of us have dreams but lack the will power to work on them.

Most people after receiving information on how to develop themselves they allow procrastination to steal it away from them, which is not the way to grow. While some let inpatient to kill theirs by preventing them to hold on and follow the procedures attached to the process of development. While some people allow themselves to be talked out of their own dream, while some allow themselves to be intimidated by lack of self-discipline and fear. That is why only few made it to the end and have the quitters to serve them as their slaves and maids.

When I came across the statement that says *"everyone can never be rich"* I was shocked, to be sincere, not that I didn't know this earlier, but there is a way you will come across some information it will sound and look strange as if you never know is a reality. This statement kept on ringing in my mind as if I never know is a statement of fac. Then I kept on asking and convincing myself that *I won't and I can't* be among those that won't make it. It became part of my mental exercises and the experience of this particular exercise I indulge in really affected me positively to the extent that every cells in me started working with the affirmation-I won't and I can't be among those that will not make it, with that my vision and goals became a powerful source of my inner energy for me to challenge myself the more.

I told myself I must be among the few that will get to the top that statement alone became path of me and a ghost hunting me till date. It became a solemn promise to self never to go back or think of quitting this can be an inspiring example for us to think about if we get tired, frustrated, or have to deal with some crisis constantly remind yourself who you aspire to be, and these are especially important when you come short. Don't end your greatness on the lips. I succeeded in convincing myself on what I want out of life, then the next question was, what are the necessary requirements for me to get there?

According to Plato, he says "the first and the best victory is to conquer self" for we are the greatest enemy of ourselves. I believe you get that clear. Throughout my years in reading the biograph of great achievers and self-made folks, I leant that it is very impossible for anyone to achieve greatness without self-discipline in other words, for you to achieve success you must embark on self-discipline which leads to self-development, because everything, including your life, your happiness, your liberty, freedom name it that you want depend on you.

So what are you waiting for? The universe is watching, waiting for you to act. GOD who sent you on this mission has already equipped you with all the necessary tools that you need to accomplish this task and excel, HE is auto of no mistakes. We begin to worry and over analyze our situations when we don't have detailed and well thought out plans for our future. Set your goals, list them down with detailed plan, according to your priority, and then take action on those ones that scares you the most. You have to exit your comfort zone if you must bring out the best in you.

We increase the existence of fear and make it bigger in our lives when we fail to do the things that frightened us. Make sure you do one thing every day. Taking meaning action towards a meaningful goals helps to paralyze our fear and give us relieve stress with huge sense of enjoyment. Overcoming your fear and anxiety spare capacity in life to focus on what you really want to be and do. Don't try to do everything at the same time set them short and long term goals starting from the ones you can achieve in one month time, three months, and six months to one year.

Pull out your calendar and make sure you are committed to it. Then your long term goals can be from a year and six months and above. With all this steps you are gradually suppressing the feeling of fear in you, and you are developing your confidence. Like Aristotle rightly said, fear is opposite of confidence. And no physical or spiritual power is against sincere effort towards achieving a well detailed plans. It doesn't matter whether what you intend to do is big or small, what matters is that you're fixing your mind through that thing daily and that keeps the mind on the track. Mind you, you are not your fears, but awareness that experience it. Step out of your comfort zone and work on becoming comfortable with the uncomfortable. Get curious about those thoughts that generate your fear, embrace it, there is no sense shying away or pretending that, that fear doesn't exist because it does.

The best way to cope with it is accepting the fact that is there and that is life. With this fact in you are buying yourself a ticket to a place you wouldn't have gone any other way, but now that you're here get the most out of it. Fear isn't designed to keep us inactive, but to help us act in a way that generate the results we need-to solve life problems. Immediately you form the habit of doing something that scares you on a daily basis, your courage grows little by little. You will agree that fear is there to expose those challenges that we need to overcome, those barriers that once were holding you back from maximizing your potential in life.

Doreen would tell herself during difficult times, "Every time I don't allow fear to keep me from doing something that scares me, I am making myself stronger and less likely to let the next fear attack stop me". Always appreciate your courage and don't fail to condemn every self-set-backs including procrastinations? Any single time you missed can never come back. Time has a great role to play in this course. You have to think and act fast.

A good friend of mine who was a banker came to a seminar scheduled and designed for entrepreneurs, I was surprise to see him there, after exchanging pleasantry, I ask him Paschal what brought you here he told me that what brought me brought him I said but you're a banker, that was then he replied at this time I noticed that he has left the world of pay-cheque. So I became more curious to know what happened and why the sudden change in decision and how the experience of leaving the banking job for entrepreneur has been all this while.

At first he told me it wasn't an easy one but he saw it as a path that will give him peace of mind and freedom, that after personal calculation that he was left with no option than to follow his mind, even though no one believed me I believe myself he said, he went on to tell me that people thought that he was going insane. So what then was your source of motivation since your people didn't believe your decision of leaving the banking system I ask him, he told me the only thing that kept him moving is the fact that he is now on the path to achieve his vision, dreams and goals, and that is what he wanted. So any other thing that comes as a result of this decision doesn't matter to me.

I ask him what exactly was your biggest challenge when you are taking this decision to tread on this path. Criticism and friends isolation he said, He told me he lost almost all his old friends including the closest ones, even some of his relatives no one want to talk to him anymore simply because he took a decision he thought that will change his life-but like I said earlier people's opinion doesn't count in my life but mine. I was shocked when he told me all these at the same time he told me that, to him it was a sign that made him to know that he has really started the journey of the great, and that gave him the courage to move on and ignore.

They're (people) going to think you are stupid. But the truth is that success is alone thing. He opted out because he didn't fit where he was coming from. Paschal said the only thing that kept him moving was the vision, dream and the goals. Until you became addicted to your vision and becoming great in life, and blind to whatever everyone is talking about you, you will continue to float around the universe aimlessly. But the amazing thing is that those people that couldn't see reason that was behind his new decision over life, those that thought he was in sane, now his successes have changed the story, things are no more as it used to be. Many of them have turned around in search of me, he said, now my success is speaking for me.

You must experience loneliness and rejections on the way, but that shouldn't bother you at all is just a sign that you have started the journey. Rejections and loneliness never make Paschal to lose focus or direction because immediately he found his destiny he found his destination and that gave him the address of where he is going and with that address on his head, people's opinion, who understand or who doesn't, does not matter to him. Until you make yourself a paramount figure, and do everything humanly possible to maintain that superiority and status you are just nothing in life. You are not a loser but when you see yourself as one you are. Just continue moving before you know it you are there.

From the moment you discover your path you discover the direction that will lead you to your destiny. You will not again be driven around like a cow and sheep that depends always on their shepherd, for everything they wanted. Commanding you on how to breathe your own breath, when to eat and how to eat, when to go out and come back, and so forth and so on. Imagine you being the master and the boss over your own life. But to get to this level you must demote some behaviors to promote some behaviors. That is the price which you need to pay-because is only a fool believes that all deserve equal rewards for unequal effort.

A seed must be separated from the rest of the seeds and buried under the soil before it can become a tree and bear fruit. And is only when a tree bears fruit it can be seen as a successful tree. If we extrapolate this to human beings, you must denounce and renounce some of your ways most especially when they have nothing in connection with your new path or the road leading to your destiny. Mind and study the kind of associate you keep, is very important to this race. Show me your friends and I will tell you who you are or what you will become.

Mind the kind of folks you share your ideas with, don't I repeat don't share your idea with low minded people because they will never see sense in what you are saying. Is like giving a dog food that was made for the kids. For you to suppress that feeling of fear, remember that humans are not born as sheep or lions but must choose a path for themselves. You have to choose your path, choose carefully the kind of people you walk with and how you spend your time because everything is built with time. The amount of time and energy you invest in yourself in that path you chose count a lots. Don't take this for granted.

Gather information on that path you want to trade on, study it, and examine the situation based on facts rather than speculation. Surround yourself with people that will inspire you, people that will make you see that your dream is not just possible but achievable. Try and avoid people that always undermine your worth those that always wish to see you under their control like a sheep been fattened on the shepherd's food-though the feeding trough of the sheep is filled, it is only with the grass and grain of its masters choosing. But these comforts bind the sheep into slavery.

I don't know what you're actually passing through right now, but one thing I know for sure is that, you are on a mission and you did not sent yourself on this mission I want you also to remember when Jesus sent out His disciples on a mission He told them do not carry anything along with you any house you come in anything they offer you take it, the same thing is applicable to your situation here, just see that state of yours now, that condition you found yourself is what your creator has for you today it is not going to be the same tomorrow, you will not continue to be there but remember a choice must to be made to attract change, the choice is yours. Because you were not born to suffer.

According to Aristotle, He states that "courage involves deliberate choice in the face of painful or fearful circumstances for the sake of a worthy goal". With this realization, Putman concludes that "there is a close connection between fear and confidence". The sacrifice of walking alone, facing rejections, taking pains from all angles like Paschal my friend and his folks against his dreams pays him in the end. HE was so obsessed, determined with burning desire to win, because he believe he were meant to be a winner not a loser nor slave to any man. Not the person they want him to be-but the person he want to be.

You don't need to worry yourself about people, you were not born to perform the same task or do exactly what they do, your nature is totally different from theirs starting from your name, the way you look, the way you think even your voice is different nobody has it the same like you in this whole wide world believe me. So trying to imitate or please them is going to be a big error disaster which you need to avoid now. You will be insulting yourself and your GOD when you look at them and want to be like them you are indirectly trying to tell GOD, HE created you without a gift or purpose.

Don't look for your gift else where your gift is within you and you will soon find it. By the end of this course you will understand why the book is called Power of Resolution. Get ready to be reformed to be formed. But before this total formation of self will be complete (like I said earlier, Power of Resolution is a book that will transform you if only you follow the exercises) you need to allow yourself to be purified by the situation for a while for your dream which is the LORD'S own project to manifest in you. If ordinary gold can be tested by fire, what much more human that worth more than gold, your endurance now is the only prove you have to show that you have faith in the journey you are about to embark on.

According to Epictetus he said, you should not be satisfied with mere learning, but add practice then training. For as time passes we forget what we learned and end up doing the opposite, and hold opinions the opposite of what we should.

COMMITMENT

Until your passion, the zeal, and the hunger to become great in you exceed the pain inflicted by your adversity you may not be successful

Anonymous

It is time to shift your attention away from distractions for permanent good, and start integrating new knowledge into your awareness of who you really are. But you cannot do this if you fail to commit yourself to it. Commitment is one of the keys to success-but to understand what the difference is between false and genuine commitment. Let's first define what we mean by "commitment", in general, this term refers to a declaration of purpose. A plan to achieve an objective, defend it and display it outwardly. Commitment is a sense of committing to that thing we know that is important to us, that thing that inspires us and that thing we believe in.

Most at times we took "commitment" for granted-without knowing how strong, effective and powerful the word is. Without serious commitment in the course of achieving your goals in life, is like forcing a cow to pass through the eye of a needle, now you can imagine how possible or impossible it is. Serious problems have been leading the lives of many down the wrong path, and believe me this wrong path will only fuel the difficulties because you can't plant apple and expect orange is not possible.

Whenever you found yourself in a path that has not be designated to you, it's as if you're walking in the dark without really knowing where you are going. But worry not yourself any more, for the compass is now with you-use it wisely. Your voluntary participation requires that you believe, know and willingly accepts to commit to the rules and regulations guiding the world of the great. Commitment indirectly means putting up the fight on what you believe, and fighting till the very end.

Your level and your strong held believe towards that vision you have is one important factor you need to look into before you can build up your level of commitment with firmness. According to Pat Riley, I quote "There are only two options regarding commitment; you're either in or you're out. There's no such thing as life in-between." Therefore, authentic commitment is not in words but in acts, and that act must start from your inner self to outside. Commitment is one of the hardest principles attached to greatness, and that is the reason why many people fall down the way. It is not easy, is hard, it takes effort, but imagine the rewards.

Before we continue, let's quickly glance on other definitions and meaning of commitment, according to Oxford dictionary it defined commitment, as the state or quality of being dedicated to a cause, activity, etc. this is a word we use often yet we don't make use of it to acquire what we want in life. This is your time to explore it. According to Pathwork guide lecture No. 196, he says that commitment means, above all, a one-pointedness of attention; giving the self in a wholehearted way to whatever the commitment may be. He was trying to let us know that, if you are committed to give your best to whatever you do, you will focus on all aspects of the subject.

Going to seminars, reading all the successful books, learning all the skills and strategies on how to make wealth, and become successful in life is a good thing, in fact is part of the journey because iron sharpens iron. But without maximum commitment to crown it, is like a student that has been attending lectures, doing his assignments, including class works, but on the day for the final exam he didn't turn up. What do you think will be the fate of that student for missing the final exams? All that you need is complete commitment towards that goals that vision that dreams, not half of it will be accomplished without full commitment. You must invest all your energies on it you don't need to shy away because that is your life.

You can never cross the sea merely by standing and staring at the water. Says Tagore, you have to step forward that is an act of commitment. Your level of commitment towards that task ahead on this new journey to greatness that you have chosen for yourself determine whether you will finally get there or not. Is a faithful dedication or obligation that binds you, your vision and goals to a particular task or course of action. That food on your table is just a good example of what we are talking about, that food on your table today is as result of the commitment of those farmers towards what they believe.

Without understanding some ancient rules that guide and governs some protocols in the universe before we came on board, it will be hard for you to know how commitment works before bringing it close to yourself. For example, before any deal is properly reached there must be an agreement between the two parties, an obligation that each party must meet in other words, each party must be committed in one way or the other in other not to breach the rule of the deal. Studies show that attachment anxiety is positively related to structural commitment, and attachment avoidance is negatively linked with personal commitment.

You should know that there is no external force other than yourself that is forcing you to do this, the only source of your energy towards commitment when the storm of trails, temptations and tribulations against your new path arises is your dreams, fix your eyes at where you are going not where you are, for where you are at the moment doesn't matter. I want you to also watch this commitment very closely since is a personal and voluntarily chosen obligation, if care is not taken it can slip through your fingers and when you lost it, the energy, time and all the invested efforts will be lost and gone.

Before that intended result of positive commitment will be achieved, there must be a strong connection between the sponsor (i.e. your enthusiasm) and the applicant (your physical commitment towards achieving that goal on the inside). The power of positive commitment start growing stronger from the moment you start asking yourself what would you like to be remembered for after this temporary life we are living? Keeping this conversation at the forefront of your mind as you continue in this journey for success will enlarge your zeal and automatically make you to know what you want and what you don't. With this perspective you will be navigating your own path.

You can't just be desiring something without committing to it. There's a big different between the two, when you simply desire something you do it only when circumstance permit, but when you're committed, you accept no excuses, only result. Without commitment your life becomes emotionally and physically still to anything worth doing. Your body is designed for adaption to adapt anything new. Is in our nature just make sure you don't break the rule of consistence, once you start introducing that new routine to the system. Your body has no option than to obey your instructions even if you don't have control over anything you're a king over your thought and actions.

Our body system is not after whether is first time or not, provided you do it repeatedly your body system will start responding and you will see yourself being more devoted, dedicated and committed. Your physical body should be a slave and a servant to your thought, by carrying out any instruction you directed it to do for the betterment of the mind and body. When you become acquainted with your vision and more committed to your goals, you're likely to be handling every challenges that could have a negative impact on the path you have chosen. Serious commitment in your area of endeavor in life will give you a sense of stability and security necessary to take risks, branch out, and grow and develop as a personality.

People get committed in one way or the other, some also commit themselves in so many things and all these varieties of commitments is aiming at one thing, which is achieving a happy and flourishing life, freedom from restriction or that good life that we desire. But often time we don't seems to be getting this desired life we admire. Why? Because we allowed the cloud of the numerous circumstances surrounding us today to cover our sense of reasoning towards making plan for the future.

We allow pressures from family, from our office, and place of work, school and in some other places we find ourselves to thwart our focus on the main thing. Quit immediately the long face and put a smiling face to attract favor, both within and outside. In this world we are today nobody cares about how you feel, because everyone is peddling with his or her own challenges. So you see, what people is looking after in you is what you are carrying, how can it solve their own problem and that is what will draw people closer to you. Like one of the bestselling author Zig Ziglar rightly said, "You can have everything in life you want, if you will just help enough other people get what they want".

When you allow your circumstance and challenges to affect your believe system, to the extent that it affect your level of commitment towards that goals that will make your tomorrow better than today, you are only ruining and judging your future negatively with present occurrences. And you have only one reward for this, which is lack in the development progress toward the path you have chosen to follow. Because your level of energy commitment will be rested on a single problematic division of labor, professional settings such as blames, criticisms, and others, rather than concentrating wholly on your own path for progress and development.

For you to make effective commitment the following factors must be fully involve, your physical energy, your mental capacities, your feelings, and the "will" to achieve success. This will must not been broken it must be protected at all cost. I believe you have heard of this old saying that says ones there is a "will" there is a way, now ask yourself do I have the will? Because is obvious that "will" is a prerequisite for a way to occur. Emotional distraction and noisy disturbance from the outside world can break this will so easily. As you are building your level of commitment is also good for you to be vigilant and avoid anything that will spoil this effort.

Committing to something you are not happy doing is a total disaster not only to your body, but also to your health, it can cause you untimely death too. And I don't need to remind you that your health is your wealth. Don't serve as a means to the end of some people who doesn't care whether you are making progress in life or not. Find time to study yourself. A man who doesn't know himself is completely lost in the crowd. Knowing who you are supposed to be your first assignment before wearing this crown of greatness.

When you study and know yourself you will not only be aware of whom you are, but also knowing your true nature and the reason why you are here on earth. You will know what you are capable and incapable of doing. You will know your weaknesses and strength, you will know the areas that you need to develop for success, and you will know what works for you and know what doesn't. Self-study is very necessary for it will clearly make you to know the exact thing you need to do at a particular time at a particular place. With self-study you will know where you are committing your energy in and why you are doing so.

Lack of this study will make you, you won't know your front from your back nor your right from your left and because you have failed to sacrifice your time to know yourself it will make you vulnerable in the sight of greedily people who use human in a ruthless manner to achieve their goals. You think it doesn't matter that is why you have be ignoring it and the result of this ignorance has been bad because you have been living a life of what goes and what life brings. For you to discover who you are, you must deny your body that unnecessary demands and take up the challenge until you arrive at your designation point with positive result.

Most people get committed to their gift or vision in life and things are moving on well with them, while some due to lack of focus they couldn't be able to identify or discover their own path. In this perplexed situation the level of our commitment coming down because it hasn't gotten any base to rest on. Now how do you know your call or identify your path? Because that is the thing you need to permanently fix and settle your commitment on to avoid fluctuating of life. Warning: never you say or join the crowd that says and have already convinced themselves to believe they don't have gift for that will permanently keep you in the dark for the rest of your life. There is power in the word, for through spoken words the universe was made.

Don't be poor and blind at the same time. Open your eyes and tap from the knowledge that refined the mind of great men and women, whom were once in the same state as you are. The nature of commitment is brought into clearer view by an examination of both the prerequisites to and effect of commitment. Very importantly for your commitment to be stronger you have to make sure that no negative feelings exist in your mind, this may sound awful, but the truth is that happiness and anger is like water and salt, light and darkness all these have nothing in common is either black or white. So is better we keep them separate the way we met them to avoid counter reactions.

You have a gift and this is how to find it because your gift is your path and unless you are on your path in this life you can't fine that joy and happiness of which you seek for, is not a curse but a fact. Avoid telling yourself that you don't have a gift, for the more you convince yourself with such words, the more you tight yourself in the bondage of poverty and slavery. At the same time locking tightly the gift instead of unlocking it. Logically if the universe was created through the spoken word of the Supreme force automatically our own words possess some potential powers to beautify our world. We shall discuss in details in our subsequent chapter the effect of words and how it affect our lives positively or negatively

How do you know you are on a right path in your life or in a path of someone else? Ok let's get down to it from here, how do you feel when that alarm wakes you up in the morning for work? How do you measure your excitement when you're leaving for work and when you're coming back? Because greatness and living a fulfilled life boils down to unlimited excitement without measure, being happy and joyous always, having your freedom without any form of restriction of any kind. Can you sincerely look yourself in the mirror and say I love my job? How is your feeling like when the weekend is coming to a close and you remember you got a job the next day? That which is taking much of your time on a daily basis are you really enjoying it? All this questions will help you to analyze your daily routine whether it matches the kind of life and happiness you wish yourself. But if it doesn't, you may likely not be in a rightful place to attract your path.

The reason why you struggle in finding your dreams and vision is because you don't get into the right mental and physical state before doing this type of process. And as soon as you get disconnected from your life's direction, other people's agendas comes before your own. Your mind must be at peace, open and alert before it can receive anything from Supreme force because your mind is the central point between you and your creator. Getting your mind arrested to be at the center is very vital and when you're in your center, you are fully present. Your mind isn't racing to the future or ruminating in the past. Instead, it's calm, empty, and alert.

Here are some tips in self-reformation process. First step, you have to create daily, a quiet and conduces environment where you can spend 15-30 minutes for yourself alone, in the cause of this self-alone, distance yourself from any form of distractions be it from human or any form of gadgets. Secondly, try and establish tranquility from inward to outside, then close your eyes and take a deep breath in and breathe out calmly, smoothly and gently. Do it repeatedly you will feel the warmth of being connected to your soul, mind and body, at this point you have summoned your whole self together. Thirdly, bring to mind that thing that each time you think about it, you feel extremely happy and wish you're already doing it or have access to it. Begin to visualize it as you close your eyes.

Why you should make this exercise a rule and do it every day until it becomes part of you is because it's easy to get distracted, to lose sight of what's important to us. If it is your first time of practicing this mental and visualization exercise you may find it uncomfortable, but don't worry before you do it one to two weeks without interruption both in the time and day you will notice change. While this exercise is going on keep one thing in mind keep visualizing a particular thing, as you are doing it get a pen and paper write down on how you wish to accomplish what you are seeing inside in real life.

Remember this is an act of revolt that is you are about taking violent action against an established way of your life. Is good and very important you know this-because the urges of your previous routine pattern of life will definitely show up. That is why you have to be prepared to turn it down. This seed you are about dusting up now was planted before your arrival on earth is just that your path in life is irrevocable. You can only leave it but no one can change it or live it if not you. When you start this exercise, you will start feeling good and happy each time you think about your life.

That place you visualize how happy you are in just seeing and feeling it in your mind is a sign you are beginning a new path of your life. And I say congratulations! In advance to you. This seed in you will bear you fruit in abundance, wealth, peace, joy and happiness, because that is your path. You're your path and your path is you and people will like you because of your originality not who you are faking to be, for no one like associating with or admire what is not real.

All these exercises and training attached to this course is necessary. Again, I will advise you to do it repeatedly until you get acquainted with the routine for accurate answer that you seek. From the moment you discover that which you want to do or that different that you want to make, write it down where you will be seeing it every day. Read it as many times as you can daily that will make you stay focused on the path. One thing you must-by all means avoid as this exercise is going on is "anger", because it attract negative energy and you don't need it, but eventually you find yourself in that mood don't waste a second in switching over to the positive energy immediately, look for something that will make you smile, laugh, or keep quiet and take a deep breathe in and exhale gently-do it three times you will return to positive energy. Do this especially if you're addicted to quick tempter.

If you're a public servant, working with people with different characters, belief with complete opposite of who you are and belief, that could be a bit challenging. But the best way to cope in that kind of environment and still maintain your emotional balance is, before you leave your home anticipate in advance that something unusual or irrational may occur at any time. Just expect unexpected as you work. This common principle prepares your feeling against anything that may occur, it balances your emotion and make it stable and you'll remain focus and committed on the task at hand. *You will in details see how to surmount your daily challenges no matter how big or small they seem to be in our subsequent chapters.*

When you find yourself in a midst of un-expectances, say lack of financial security, unsecured job, uncoordinated company or organization, poverty, or in any hardship-just remember, there is a sequence in achieving progress, that level you are now is a bridge which you must pass before you see yourself on the other side. The past, present and the future are naturally interconnected, so is inevitable. The energy you attract to yourself at this point, be it negative or positive determines how your next will be. At this stage your brain is at the sharpest level to produce lasting and favorable solutions to that problems-if only you properly channel the energies well.

Are you still doubting yourself? Are you still confused on what to decide on? Are you still depending on human to make ends meet? Are you still afraid to make a commitment towards what you believe? Do you deplore your weakness, your lack of self-assertion? All these only have one thing to bring to you which is intentional negative reactions in your system, and the reflection of this feeling on the outside will be the exact copy of what is going on the inside of you. And when you allow this to continue in this direction it will lead you to destruction, it will make you weak, anxiety, lack of assertiveness and all these ills are what you want to free yourself from.

When you are doing something that's out of the ordinary, the paradigm will try and stop you. But, if you want to win, you have to keep moving. Pathwork said in his lecture that u can only be free from this kind of situations if you genuinely establish a connection between them and their cause, the negative intention, so that the latter can be given up.

As you're going with commitment to what you believe you are unmasking complacent, fear, worry, anxiety, insecurities, self-doubt, mental hurry and self-loathing and the result is keeping you unstuck, unlocking yourself from the box of stagnation, starved of your dreams and ambitions.

In other for you to commit and remain committed to anything you wish to see yourself succeeding in doing, you have to anticipate temptations-that may tempt you to quit half way. This feeling will keep you prepared to surmount whatever that may come in-between your decision. This challenge is inevitable it must surely come after you to test your ability. That is why is very important to know what triggers your commitment with that you will reprogram your time, and know where you're channeling your energy for effective result. Because every effort invested has a reward waiting for it.

Therefore you need to keep your commitment on track to remain fresh in your mind and body this tracking process doesn't apply only to great and significant ventures but also in your spiritual path of self-evaluation, which is the most important undertaking in life at large. This tracking process will also help you in monitoring the level and the growth of your commitment to that goal, to know if you are falling behind or making progress. This tracking method will guide your steps each day until that goal is accomplish.

It is also important that you are consistent. Nothing is worse than a behavior or habit that is inconsistent and not comprehensive. The effective steps you need to take to make sure that your effort towards that thing you want to achieve is to define thoroughly the targeted goal for the day and how much energy and time that are needed to invest on it. When you define your mini daily goal, it will channel your focus, energy and time to that project at hand. With this step you can be able to say by the end of the day this is the percentage of the energy or this is the number of hours I sacrificed in this project today.

Decompose your numbers (hours) for the day, fix the hours according to your schedule to ensure the accomplishment of that goal. This process will make you to know how, when, where, and who you spend your precious time with. It will make you to see that each hour of the day is accounted for in terms of those tasks you have set. Your breakdown plans in achieving your goals should be based on the time frame that you set a night before, as well as your normal routine for the day. One good thing I observed when I took commitment as a serious business is that it helps me to re-coordinate myself completely, both the way I think, behave, and see things around with a positive view.

Immediately you see the light of a new dawn, start the day with the plans you made a night before, start controlling your steps by telling yourself things that you need to accomplish today and that you are not ready to take any excuse but result, with this thought in your mind you have started the tracking process. Don't slack in seeking out for information and data, the information and the data you collect today is a tool for future battle so don't take it for granted. Any information, data you are gathering is for the sake of where you are going, they are all sequence of success.

For you not to feel disappointed or dismay in the course of commitment you need to be conscious of checking yourself every minute of the day. Usually people give only half of themselves and are then confused, vexed, and disappointed when the result is accordingly incomplete. Even if you're surrounded by fake people, don't get discouraged and definitely be careful not to let them rub off on you. If you imitate them, you'll be giving in to hive mentality where you let others think for you. And that is not how to live I said it before and I will repeat it again, don't serve as a means to an end of other people. A personal commitment with a link to a new found path is heading to victory. But a commitment to other people's opinion is a slavery.

Choose a cause, a personal cause and fight for it. And you should, first of all, be committed to it-knowing that you have rights and that you deserve happiness and success. That dream of yours is 100% possible if only you agree with me right now that it is, yes I repeat if only you believe it is, your believe is the only passport that you need to bring it to reality because HE who shows you the vision is all knowing. Abraham in the Bible obeyed when he was called to go out to a place that he was to receive as an inheritance. And he went out not knowing where he was going. That is an act of faith and commitment.

His faith and believe pushed him into commitment. That vision and that dream of yours is your own inheritance from the most High GOD, you will be wasting your time waiting to see the details on how to commit yourself in actualizing that dream, because you won't get its details until you make a move. Read, make a research, and ask questions on how it can be done from people you know and trust who have passed through and still on the same lane. Fill yourself with the knowledge of where you want to go. Keep the picture alive in you do a thing every day that links to that dream all these are parts of the commitment.

Have you allowed the transition of money to hinder you from taking a step or towards that dream? Remember money is merely paper and numbers that are traded for a person's time and effort. With effort, poverty is impermanent. Is better to suffer today as a result of your commitment towards achieving that dreams and goals and be good tomorrow, than to remain uncommitted today and die in prison of your misery tomorrow. This change is not easy, but it is worth it-and the results are lasting. Develop harmony within your mind and what you think and do.

Your intense commitment towards your believe, and goals must be challenged to confirm your believe. It may be difficult at times, the meaningful pursuits of life are hardly ever easy. Therefore, find encouragement to stay committed on your goals and to your vision and very soon you will see that it all worth the challenge. Remember, is not possible for everyone to be great or successful, that is why in every contest there is always a winner and a loser, but I know you won't be a loser because you have been equipped and still tapping from the knowledge that will make you emerge as a winner.

According to Vince Lombardi "Most people fail not because of a lack of desire but because of a lack of commitment". So chose, commit and expect your winning report card.

HABIT

I will form good habits and become their slave. And
how will I accomplish this difficult feat? Through these
scrolls it will be done, for each scroll contains a principle
which will drive a bad habit from my life and replace it
with one which will bring me closer to success

OG Mandino

Before we begin our studies on this chapter, I want you to critically
confront yourself with the following questions like, on whose brain am I
cultivating my time and energy on? Is it taking me to my own promising
land or their own promising land for continuity of my slavery to them?
On whose idea have I been living for years now? What is behind the delay
of exploration of my own latent? How long will I continue wallowing on
peoples thinking, opinions over my life? When will I start giving attention
to my intuition? Will I die making others happy and go sad? By following
them like a sheep without a shepherd? When will I stop embarrassing my
Maker, myself by ignoring my instinct?

Drinking this questions like a class of cold water will form internally
a new perspective view of who you are, where you are and what your
next action will be. Because your brain which is the processing unity of
your body plays a key role in translating the content of your mind (your
thought, feelings, attitudes, memories and imagination) into complete
pattern that is seen in this play through the way you live your life. For you
to experience a different transformation your thought need to be soaked
deeply into some certain facts that will influence your pattern style of
living.

Until you face yourself with these life changing questions above and ready to react on them you can never develop that existing hidden latent talent in you. This latent is like a hungry lion which has been caged for years inside of you by you, is roaring in you waiting for your permission to come out. But you allowed your current situation to serve as an excuse for you not to react on it release, listen, who has been destined to fail will always have excuses for not doing a thing. This is a wakeup call for you, there is no time to waste any more. The only thing suitable and qualified to bring your latent into development or manifestation is only that current circumstance you are sitting on right now.

Until you get to the apex of this level of thinking and reasoning you will not see the need for self-transformation into another new realm of your life. And this can only be achieved through initiation of new habit and eliminating the old ones that has not helped you in any way but wasting of time, energy and resources. Before you solve a problem you must know the root of it. See, you have to disassociate your thinking from this general dogma that without money you can't do anything, though I was blindly following that dogma for years, but when I started reading good books, my thinking developed. For example money can't think for you at any situation, money cannot tell you how to respond to any challenge. You are not made to serve money remember but money was created to serve you.

Before I share my experience with you over my dependence on money for everything in my life, including my happiness before I got internal liberation. I will like us to quickly look into the word habit and see what most people have been missing, thinking that money is the cause of their problems. According to Oxford Bibliographies they said, the concept of habit refers to routine behavior which is based on repeated exposure to same kinds of environmental cues. These cues lead to an automatic association with the cue and the behavior that follows irrespective of whether a desired goal is reached.

The American Journal of Psychology (1903) defines a "habit", from the standpoint of psychology, as a more or less fixed way of thinking, willing, or feeling acquired through previous repetition of a mental experience. According to Meriam-Webster, habit is a behavior pattern acquired by frequent repetition or physiologic exposure that shows itself in regularity or increased facility of performance. Now if you observe from this different definitions of habit from these authors and scholars you will agree with me that habit is a manifestation of what we think and believe and do repeatedly that forms our behavior which is the habit.

It all boils down to what we have acquired through previous repetition of a mental experience. That is why I said money has nothing to do with the way we think or feel and respond to the environmental cues rather it depends on our internal perspective of things. When I finish my college I was having this mind-set that money is all that I need to be happy in life and that is final for me then, there is nothing anybody can say that can change that believe I was having, behold that thought stick and it really affected me so badly to the extent that I found no joy in anything around me, and I was having zero account.

But when I finally got a job, my account changed from zero to figures at some point I still found myself very sad and angry that was when I ask myself what is really going on with me? I flashed my memory back I remember when I was searching for job when I had no money on me and all my believe then for not being happy was because of my brokenness, but now I have job and I have the money why then am I still sad? That was when I came to understand that money, fame wealth, position, power all these are transient and man should not depend on them for happiness.

So I discovered that my unhappiness mood which I use to experience some time is as a result of my mental programed attitude which exclusively controlled my habitual behavior from being happy with my life. And the quest to change the paradigm became very intense on me. A good number of people out there today still believe and blame the lack of money in their pocket as a result of their misfortune and unhappy life. Most at times we don't know why we react or do what we do at times. Paradigms are a multitude of habits passed down from generation to generation.

We all were once during our childhood experience mental colonization from our parents, guardian, and groups. And as a child we were, we are handicap completely that's ok, but as an adult you need to understand that a lot of things have changed. And as a human you need to upgrade yourself to match up with the uncountable challenges that due face man on a daily basis. Though it's not easy, but when you remember how badly it has been, and how worst it will become if nothing urgent is done and the result you will get if you strain yourself a little bit, you will know truly it's worth it.

Old habits are hard to break and new habits are hard to form because the behavioral patterns which humans repeat become imprinted in neural pathways, but it is possible to form a new habit through repetition and regular practice which has to start from the way you view yourself, the way you think, your environment, the world and opportunity. In elimination of the old habit for the new one to come first, you have to pencil down the old habits that need to be change, at the same time convert those time you spent on them each day most especially when they have no link to your dreams.

Initiating a new habit is not an issue, anyone can do that but where the problem lies is maintaining it. For any habit to form and stick, there must be a base or purpose of which that habit is initiated on. You need to know what triggers you to initiate that habit, you need to know why and define it very clearly that-will serve as a shell in time of trials on the way. Because some of the habits most of the people exhibit today are based on purpose, which some don't care to know and we end up not finding result for our own gratification. But how can you get a result that will favor you on a plan someone initiated? That result you are expecting is going into the pocket of the initiator(s) as a reward for that behavioral pattern of which you are following.

Two hundred years have passed since 1807, when a universal ban on human trafficking was declared. Yet despite the fact that slavery is illegal all over the world, it is alive and flourishing more than ever. The conditions of today's slaves are not that much better than in the past, and often, slavery today is much worse than the slavery of the past. What is slave? Simply put one who is wholly subjected to the will of another, one who has no freedom of action, but whose person and services are wholly under the control of another. One who has lost the power of resistance, one who surrenders himself to any power what so ever.

Generally, slavery is ascribed to people lacking freedom who do not receive wages for their work, but today slavery frequently includes receiving wages for performing tasks that are exhausting, humiliating and dangerous. This is more reason why your core aim should be on focusing deeply in fighting for freedom in order to live a free conscience life. By breaking down bit by bit any habit that is still holding you down, not to become a slave to your own passion in life. Progress start from that very moment you know what you want to do and ready to do it and doing it become success in progress, finished become success accomplished.

Let me bring a clear view of what you want to do in your mind. I want you to see every reason why you should not mind any challenge that may be standing your way for success. The life of abundance is what you grow up to see that is necessary for anyone who is dreaming to be free from lack and want, from restrictions of any kind. You are trying to break a chain of lack and want, restrictions, rejections, disappointments, misfortune, disgrace, chain of failure, reproach, any hard lock all of it have been on ground before you came on board and because you are not comfortable with them you deemed it fit to pass judgment against them to be free.

So for you to remain strong in tackling these problems which has been there for ages before you, is enough reason for you to know that this chain of which you want to cut is hug and thick-so don't expect it to be an easy move, because if it were to be an easy move as most people out there think, the road could have been cleared before you came. So get ready to see hard, embrace it for that is the only thing that will separate you from others. Never you blame yourself again for anything, because it is not your fault that you want to clear up this mess of ugly life that you met on your way in life.

Don't pity yourself one bit because is a way your brain is trying to make you feel weak, and weakness bring depression of the spirit and when you allow your spirit to be defeated you can't be strong enough to face that challenge. Always ask yourself why am I struggling this way? What exactly is your target? Convince yourself that the pain on you now is the price for the victory ahead. Always remind yourself that you're on a transformation wheel and anything that stands on the way becomes the way and you are not ready to quit or go back because you have come a long way.

By now I believe you might have understand clearly without any single doubt that every habit, behavior, or character was design or formed based on purpose and intentions. A lot of people copy's people's habit or behavior without knowing the reason why that habit was initiated by the initiator. Some habit is inherited or transferred dogma. This is time to sieve those unfavorable habits for favorable habits to take place. But that will be on one condition that is if you really want to achieve success in any area you are dreaming to achieve success in.

The speed of which you applied in developing this new habit pattern, largely determined by the intensity of the emotion that accompanies the decision to begin acting in a particular way. Are you acting based on your own instinct or based on people's opinion because you need to understand this very clearly, every action has a benefit and reward, so if your action depends largely on the account of people, organization, group or that individual you are copying then they will be the beneficiary of the reward. You need to know this to enable you to know where your energy and effort is going, so that you will know the kind of reward you are expecting instead of wasting time being a slave indirectly in another man's idea.

When initiating a new habit it is not really necessary letting everyone to know about it. But incase and for the fact that you still have some good ones who share the same view in your group team, organization that may be thinking in opposite direction as a result of your new found habit, try and clear their mind, for them to understand and make some necessary adjustment in the time you people share together, with this the union will not be hot or experience separation as a result of your newly initiated behavior for a better tomorrow.

There are strong correlation between certain habits and being successful. Why? Because many habits fall in line with values that can help you become successful. Developing a habit that will contribute to your success is what I am talking about here. What you desire in life should be the foundation of your habit. You have to understand there is a process in progress in anything happening under the universe. The people that value freedom and autonomy are the ones who strive to any length to achieve their desire.

Any habit that are aiming to a greater success should always align with things that are related to the goal. Every habit is initiated to satisfy crave through response of reaction towards getting a result that has a link to the cue. This paradigm resetting is what you need to get your new habit moving and you need to set it based on your own goal and aspirations. Initiating a concept that will bring you into the realm light of a new behavior to cover the old pattern of habit and discover your own habit that will lead you to that life time expectancy.

Investing in what you believe is one sure way of getting you to your dream. Because where you constantly channel your attention shapes the way you view things in reality and that deepens your understanding in what you are doing. For the sake of clarity, I would want us to quickly do this little calculation together. I want you to use it and access the way you spend your time on a daily basis it'll help you to know if you're being productive for yourself with your time or not. Because the way you manage your time in the field of success determine how far you will go.

You will agree with me that we all, both the rich and the poor share the same equal time, the same twenty four hours each day. Let say you spend eight hours at work, eight hours at night sleeping, making it 16 hours already gone, and out of 24 hours you're left with extra eight hours, how do you spend it? I also know you have families, loved ones, friends, relative, social media to respond to and some other things we sacrifice our time for. Now remember this calculation is just a clue for you to fix your eyes on what is consuming your time whether it worth it or not because that is where the formation of habit start after defining the purpose.

Time is one commodity most valuable on earth. Let's say you have a total of five hours as a left over time each day, is a small figure right, but if you multiple it by 31days that make up one month, it will give you 155 hours. Can you tell yourself that this time has been efficiently used in approaching my goal, my passion and my aspiration that I have inside or have I just wasted it unproductively on things that are no way related to my goals. The day you came on earth and the day you will die that gape in the middle is the most important period of your life that will tell the world that you once lived by living and not just existing.

It is very clear that when you don't own your time and schedule people will help you own it by controlling it for you. I remember when I was floating around like a balloon on the surface of the earth walking aimlessly people were busy taking advantage of that, making a decision for me, determining what should be in my life. Deciding for me but thanks be to GOD Almighty for showing me my path. Through reading good books, and associating with the right people my life was positively affected and that redirected my world completely. So whether it is your meeting calendar, daily or weekly goals, projects, or your weekend plans, if you're not taking charge of them, then you're left with no option than to accept what is being planned on your behalf or get frustrated.

For you to be faithful to yourself and manage your time effectively you need to develop the habit of making use of the TO-DO-LIST that is if you have not been doing it. It helps you to keep yourself on check, whether you are doing what you have mapped out to do for the day or you are going astray. It will also keep you on top of the game by gradually helping you to actualizing your daily goals. It give me joy when I cross things on my to- do-list showing that a particular task(s) has been accomplished. It's a very satisfying part of the process.

Develop the habit of reading for at least 1 hour daily until your body masters the new routine-to the extent that you no longer check the time you spend in reading. Like me now, reading has always been on top of the list of my hobbies. I feel like something is missing in me or that am missing one important information that will be useful to me in future. I can't stay for complete two hours without reading something, that habit is still alive till date. Some people wonders and ask what has reading of books got to do with acquisition of wealth? In fact let me tell you-that is where the secrets of success are hidden.

Success are hidden in the pages of books. Warren Buffet one of the richest men in the world today says he reads about 600 pages every day can you imagine that. Rich people makes reading a solid habit. When I was forming this particular habit of reading it was very difficult in the beginning because it consumes time and energy. But the truth is that it forced me to readjust my time and invest more in developing my zeal in search of knowledge and wisdom. This daily practice in reading especially finding out what differentiate the poor from the rich.

I want you to know that your life today is essentially the sum of your habits. How happy you are or unhappy, how successful you are or unsuccessful it all boils down to your previous routine behaviors done on a regular basis. It's a recurrent and often unconscious patterns of behavior which you acquired. How you constantly and repeatedly behaves i.e. what you spent your time thinking, doing each day automatically forms who you are including what you believe and the personality that you portray.

Sticking tightly to a routine pattern of life will keep you focused and it will allow you to engage in the things that will bring success to you. Transferring from old habit to new habit can be challenging but if you must know the truth that is where the growth lies, winners start winning when they start resisting pains and challenges and kept on moving forward in the face of adversity, while the losers loose-out in the face of adversity, pains and challenges. That is why I want you to embrace the challenge just bear it in mind that the challenge has not come to stay but to train you and leave. Is not easy, is hard, greatness is not for the weak minds, and every effort has a reward.

Keep pushing forward, if you are tired rest, take a short break tiredness is not laziness nor act of quitting. Before you make your habit stick you have to convince yourselves beyond every reasonable doubt why you are forming that habit. This will make you to withstand any storm or obstacles that may be coming to pull you down or set you back to your old pattern of habit that has nothing to offer you but failure and perpetual pain and suffering. That is why is very important to set your mind straight towards your goal and remain unbreakable towards that, don't confuse who you are with what you do.

If forming a habit that will bring you success in life is easy, everyone would have been rich, but because is hard, that is why only the strong conquers it all. Keep your mission in mind always through mental exercise via affirmation. Affirmation is a very powerful way of which you can use and connect tightly to your subconscious for easily manifestation of your dreams. Affirmation will support and encourage you in the middle of adversity. Affirmation also hold a key to unlocking the law of attraction and creating the life of your dreams.

Affirmation is one of the habits we hold tightly to heart. I don't joke with it. In fact, whenever am affirming sometimes I get carried away and forgot am in the public. Some of my colleagues will think am mad or in sane, but the truth is that I don't care what anyone or anybody says or talk about me. My only concern is what am doing and people is free to think as they wish to. Is a strong habit you wouldn't avoid on this journey. Successful people around the world hold this very firm. The technique you use to do this begins with daily affirmations, which are simple statements that describe a goal in its already complete state.

What is your habit? I want you to know that you are designing your future and the future of your unborn generations with that habit, for you to form a habit that will link you up with your dream goals you must be willing to learn and follow the footprint of those (high achievers) who have passed there before you and that got to do with the way you manage your time from now. Doing the same thing day after day is fine, as long as that routine of habits push you to be your most productive and healthy self. You must learn how to stop tolerating your old behavior that is if, you want it to give way for the new one to come in and operate in you for effective result. Because what you don't tolerate is what you hate and what you hate you don't have any business with it.

Sometimes you get yourself entangled with multiple of tasks each day, most times you end up not accomplishing even one of them, this doesn't really help you or anyone else get anything done. In a case like this you have to adopt the system compartmentalization, in that way you could be able to differentiate these streams of thought or activity to reduce the transition time between the many things you need to get done. Visualizing and setting mental goals for the day, week, month and even several months and then creating deadlines to accomplish them.

I also make sure in the course of achieving my daily goal I wear a smiling face. This single habit attract a lot of success to me, you can also try attaching smiling as you form your habit. When I started practicing the habit and following the steps of the most influential and successful people, I see myself being deeply immersed in an activity to the extent that all my mental chatter disappears, and I stop having self- referential thoughts. In my quest of self-development through habits for exponential growth, I noticed that great people don't harbor chaos and they are always proactive and organized.

If being appreciative is not yet in your habit try and add it, because for anything you receive no matter how small be thankful. Is a positive reinforcement that opens doors for lots of favors. This is one of the greatest habit, but looks very common in the eyes of many. Make it part of your habit and the benefit is unimaginable. The power of your habit controls your destiny, and for you to control your destiny through your habit you need to start controlling the amount of time you spent consuming other people's creativity. Yes very important, my father ones told me son, don't score 3/7 instead score 7/3.

For example how many hours do you spend on social media each day? How many hours do you spend watching television, I said it before we have the same equal hours daily and no one gets extra hours from anywhere. How can you dedicate yourself in creating your own wealth when you are using the same time in dedicating on others creativity? The secret of forming habit is this-when you sacrifice more time in trying to create something other people will consume you will have little or no time left to pay attention to anything else other than the things you have mapped out to do. Successful people discipline themselves not to be addicted to things that doesn't bring promotion into their life.

When you don't have time to create something significant for yourself, am sorry riches may be far from you. Like Warren Buffet rightly said, "If you don't find a way to make money while you sleep you will work until you die". You must have enough courage to hate yourself to suffer to create the kind of life you want for yourself if you love yourself. Note if you die today is you that died, if you live is still you that lives, so you have to take 100% responsibility of your life and the result. I also believe you have heard that before but the question is does it really sink down well inside of you?

Life is too rugged it doesn't joke with anyone, so joke not with your life and success. It doesn't matter what your condition is, where you are now you can still create, achieve what you want and become a champion since you're still breathing and reading this book. This could only be possible if you give up all the excuses why you are not progressing and stop complaining and find a way. Always make sure that the foundational habit is very strong and solid because that is where other habits will flow from. If the foundation is not strong enough it won't protect or carry the building.

Your life is a product of your values not your feelings, your life is a product of your decisions not your conditions, you need to understand that the life you are living today is a function of your feelings, your mood, your impulses, other people's treatment and for you to turn things around to be in the shape that you want it to be, you have to be willing to take responsibility and that is the bottom principle of being reactive. And if you don't or ignore this responsibility and duty over your life you will be a product of the past and that is a bad habit and it won't take you anywhere instead it keeps you in the past.

Principles of life is the order of the universe, you can't disagree with it you can't ignore it, you can neglect it, you can turn your back at it but you can't disagree with it. When you discipline yourself for a particular purpose you form a habit that becomes your law, that becomes your principle and a person with character does not live on what is popular, they live on their principle. Don't be confused with crowd or people's general concept of your life, rather live based on your own principle(s). For you to safe guide your future and your destiny you need to protect your character, your habit because character simple means that which is unchanging.

People cannot trust you if they found out that you lack character, your character attract loyalty character is a commitment to a set of values without compromise. Don't violate the standard you have set for yourself, don't let anything to come in between your policy. You have to lock yourself up in the room of your conviction and throw away the key and become a slave to your habit. Remember we said earlier that habit is what you constantly do to integrate your thoughts, your words, and your actions to become one powerful force. In fact your habit is a sacrifice for principles.

You can't just say I want it, you don't just wish it, but acting it day after day, weeks after weeks, month after months, and year after years then you can beat your chest in sincerity and say yes I am doing it. This is the only thing that separate you from the crowd. That is your life and that is who you are. You don't think what they think, you don't sleep when they sleep, and you wake up before everyone else, because you're what you constantly do. Now let me get this straight, if you really want to be rich (when I mean rich, I don't just mean excess cash in your pocket only, but rich life, freedom, spending time with family, free for choices, free to do whatever you want to do at your own convenience without any restriction isn't that what you want?) you must learn to dominate.

Your thoughts, your feelings and emotion towards wealth and riches will only be there, but your reasoning which is part of your mental habit, resulting in attitudes and actions towards that thought is the only way to bring that thought into reality, and the fastness of the manifestation of thought turning into reality depends on the level of motivation, and the force of friction associated with your habit. When you understand and work in harmony with the universal principles that lead you directly to the source of all life's riches, your results are predictable.

Success depends on previous preparation, and without such preparation failure is assured.

MIND CONTROL

*The mind is just like a muscle the more you exercise
it, the stronger it gets and the more it can expand.*

Idowu Koyenikan

You need to know the power of your arsenal before you can boast for war, if not your enemy will eat you up in the battle field. Do I need to tell you that if that is the case, you're automatically defeated? The superior man is distressed by the limitations of his ability; he is not distressed by the fact that men do not recognize the ability that he has. You need to observe and know how your body system operates, is obvious many don't know this but when you know and master it, you won't be falling into some of the problems you often found yourself sometimes-in life. For you to gain control over your mind, that is prevailing over your flesh not the other way round you must be in spirit to control the flesh.

What you're about to control is non-physical, your mind is a spiritual force that controls almost everything that is happening in your life. And for you to be in charge of this mind you have to be willing to obey the laws of nature. Everyone has this will power to tackle and win this battle of survival call life which we all found ourselves in. No one is left out without mind, so no one was created empty handed either, for GOD is not daft and HE can't make such expensive mistake-knowing how rough the ground where he sent you is.

Mistakes are for we mortal (humans) because of our imperfection in nature. The problem you face at times is that, you allow the noise of the environment and the inner conflict to take over your mind, and when this happens you find it difficult to ascertain your inner voice for direction and guide over some critical issues. At first life is what you feel it is that is what it will appear to you because it will be moving with your thought and your thought direct your actions and your actions are who you are.

We all have mind but because of the ignorance on how to use this powerful weapon, we feel empty. You are like salt that every cook needs to make his food tasty, that is how the world needs your dreams, and that your unique innovation to be complete, because that is why you are created in the first place not to copy anyone. But when the salt loses its flavor, how then shall it be seasoned, don't feel quilt for anything-for the people who sat in darkness have seen a great light through what you are reading. Don't be left out for the people around you need to see that light shining on you, don't disappoint yourself and those that are looking up to you.

In the cause of reading this book you will discover and be enlightened on how powerful your mind is, but don't regret why you haven't notice or use it all this while. For everything under the universal order is programmed to happen in due time. So believe this is just the perfect time to know it.

Knowing is one thing, putting in practice
what you know is another thing

Anything that takes your attention or focus away has succeeded in disaccustoming the force of your creativity. Your goal your dream and your aspirations should be what you are living for. You should be ready to avoid and attack back, anything that may want to take this focus away from you and resist it by all means. It sound very simple but is heavy when it comes to implementation, because it will demand a lot of sacrifice-that will make you look like the highest fool on earth, is a sacrifice that will make you look as if you don't have sense at all, is a sacrifice that pains so deeply to the heart when demonstrating it. Is all about ignoring things that doesn't matter, is all about overlooking ordinary things that people around you normally wouldn't have ignored if they were you.

Always remember, ignorance is not an act of fear it simply means you refuse to get acquainted to distraction or notice it. This is an act of wisdom for the things ahead of you. Your mind is the only passport you need for creation. And before you access this mind for creativity, it is important that you observe the law of harmony, this law of harmony is a supreme potential of balance and when you walk with this law you can be assured of adventure positive outcome of controlling your own mind, but when the law transgress be assure of suffering.

When it comes to creativity your mind is powerless if is in the state of chaos and restlessness. Many people feel frustrated in life, many don't know the next direction to take, and some are lost in total confusion. The world we found ourselves is full of war, fighting here and there, no money to take care of the family, no job for young graduate, and no peace. All these happenings, sometimes affect our inner peace and that makes us lose control of ourselves some times. Despite all these I still want you to understand that you in particular, did not invent any of these things that have taken the order of the day.

The inventor(s) of all those restlessness in this world should be more worried not you, on the contrary you should know that some people have been destined to distort and interrupt the peace and the spirit of focus that has been instilled in you. And when this is achieved, you are no different from them, you are lost like them, confused like them frustrated and walking like aimless ghost like them. That is why for the sake of your dreams try as much as you can to ignore any form of distraction both external and internal. See I understand you can't stop completely at once the feelings of negative, or other unhallowed thoughts coming into your mind, but the truth is that you can't stop flies from flying over your head but sure, you can and I repeat you can stop them from perching.

Negative thought sometimes seems to be the only thing that comes our mind most especially when we fail or face disappointment or pains, never the less I have some good news for you, worry no more. But do you know that you can never know the full size of a balloon until you pump air into it-and that is exactly how human beings are in nature. Human nature is powerful, the same way other species are powerful in their own way. And you can never know this until you stretch yourself, you won't know how powerful and how strong you are.

The problem with some of us human is that we easily get distracted, either by external source or internal source. And this as a result of lack of ability to pay attention or lack of interest and believe in what we say we want to do. The common factors that distract people with low self-esteem is the crowd, environment, friends, relatives, and immediate family or even colleagues in the office. But the truth is that for the sake of your dreams, goals and for the fact that you need concentration to accomplish them, you need to identify your distractions and put a full-stop to all of them. That is if you really want to get there soon.

In controlling your mind for a positive result, it is necessary you familiarize yourself with and get used to positive attitudes, rather than negative attitude and feelings. Many do not know that our habituations to bad emotions, such as hatred, envy, jealousy, wickedness, greedy, fear of unknown makes a huge obstacle in achieving our own personal goals and aspirations. Thus, we need to identify the various forms of bad afflictive emotions and combat them right on the spot. If you gradually become accustomed to controlling bad attitudes, over a period of time it is possible even for someone who after used to get very angry to become calm and calmness is what your mind need to function effectively for your benefit.

Before we continue further, I would want us to quickly glance through this word called "mind" to know exactly what we are talking about. Because you need to know the nature of what you are about to control before you can be absolutely in charge of it. The mind, what comes to your head whenever you hear the word mind? And what has knowing it got to do with you, you may be tempted to ask, all these and more will be our focal point as we roll down to this chapter, because is not all about controlling what comes and goes out of our mind, but also analyzing how things works in there. With that knowledge you can be able to know how to use what you have got for your own good.

Mind is usually defined as the faculty of an entity's thoughts and consciousness. It holds the power of imagination, recognition, and appreciation, and is responsible for processing feelings and emotions, resulting in attitudes and actions. In other words your mind is the set of cognitive faculties which include your consciousness, thinking, perception, judgement, language and memory. I told you earlier that you have all it takes to become who ever that you want to become on earth. All you need to do is to believe. And I think this is the most and simplest of it all, just to believe and have faith that your wish is possible and you will wake-up one morning and see your dream standing beside you.

You are too powerful to bow down to that mere challenge believe me, Power of Resolution has come to rekindle your forces, your imagination power, and your perception to make changes in your way of life through your way of reasoning and thinking. The existence of the mind is like that of gravity and electricity that can only be inferred from its physical effects. The way we react and respond to issues and things that are happening around us. The mind is the element of a person that enables him to be aware of the world and their experiences to think, and to feel. Is the faculty of consciousness and thought Says Professor Mark S. the lead of educator of the University of Cape Town.

Learning how to stimulate the communication between your conscious and the subconscious minds is a powerful tool on the way to success, happiness and riches. There are two kind of practices which has to do with mental exercise you have to know this if you are willing to indulge in it, I experienced it and is awesome. Is non-cognitive and cognitive exercises. During a non-cognitive exercise you train your mind to act implicitly and automatically in the right ways. While during cognitive exercise you're meant to utilize your reasoning capacities to think through a given issue in an explicit and rational way.

These two exercises are legitimate and you can use them to increase your mental antifragility. Is obvious that we are raised in a society that values ornamentation, so it may be tricky to rid ourselves of that desire. But you should also know that those who want more than what they need and what they have will always want more, and this only leads to a cycle of dissatisfaction. And this is the reason why we lack control over our mind and body because if you are miserable with yourself, you will be miserable wherever you go. On top of being happy with the essential developing our inner self is the key.

Your subconscious mind is a data bank for everything that you do, which is not in your conscious mind. Your subconscious stores your beliefs, your previous experience, your memories, also your skills. Everything that you have seen, done or thought is also there. It constantly monitors the information coming from the senses for dangers and opportunities. And it would communicate that information to the conscious mind. It is very clear that mind and body denote the problem that we inherited on this earth, because we all were born problem free-but as we grow, we began to acquire them through thought and the way we view ourselves and things around us.

Resetting your mind is like when you take yourself to the gym, everything lies in your mind and your respond to event. That is why you have to be willing to follow the regular routine of this whole mental exercise to ensure that your aim is accomplished in no distance time. Avoid multiple signal coming from your conscious down to your subconscious mind, sometimes when our subconscious receives different kinds of signals from conscious mind it get confuse on the one to work on as our priority and it affect the response we ought have gotten when we make a request. For example, you call a small boy to help you purchase something from the nearby store, on his way going, you changed your mind on what he will buy immediately you call him back, and tell him the changes then send him back, as he is going you called him back again for the second time to the extent that you called him back for the third time, now imagine if you were the boy, what will be your mind towards this man who is sending you on this errands?

This is exactly what our subconscious mind suffer From some of us sometimes. Sometimes our indecisiveness is mainly our problem, you want "A" today, tomorrow you want "B" next you want "C". I am not trying to discourage you or speak against your multiple task no, but what I am trying to make you to understand here is that try to be specific in your demand, set your demand straight and make it clear be more specific-based on your priority. When you accomplish "A" then channel your focus on "B", that is how the law of attraction works if you really want to achieve success.

Your subconscious mind is the most powerful tool you have and is always there as long as you keep breathing it keep working for you taking whatever you ordered it to do. It can never reject or forget your orders rather you do, because when you fail to communicate frequently with your mind, to provide you with an idea on how to get your orders. Because the work of your subconscious is not just to take your orders but also make sure that your orders are delivered to you but unfortunately this cannot happen without your maximum attention to the request you make this is where self-believe and faith sets in.

This unique mechanism planted in your body called mind is in charge to bring your thought into reality, is part of you and is you. That is why is very important you learn how to use it, and learning how to use it is a task that needs constant communication between you and your subconscious. That is taking control of your mind in fact, research on self-determination theory demonstrates that the more you feel you're in control of your circumstances, the more productive and fulfilled you're likely to feel. And this lead to serious habit of meditation. Turning this mental thought into habit, taking it as a pills every day without cease until the whole cells in you masters it.

Remember not to focus in trying to know "how", all you need is to form and keep forming the picture of where you are going in mind, while you physically work towards achieving that dreams. Unfortunately, your subconscious doesn't understand language, making it difficult to influence. What it does understand are images, emotions, and feelings especially under certain-this is why athletes and high performers spend time visualizing success. Have you experienced this in your life before-there is this particular issue you have been thinking on how to solve but you couldn't be able to figure it out and you left it aside working on other projects at hand, then one day all of a sudden the solution to that particular problem that you left aside pops into your head. And you're like why didn't I think of this before now.

That is your subconscious at work, that problem you lodged in for years, months, weeks, days ago is there processing. Your subconscious mind will continue to work on that task long after you leave it, this is known as incubating the problem. During this incubation your subconscious will continue to work on the original challenge. That is why visualizing that dream always as if is already accomplished task is another powerful way to influence your subconscious in generating ideas for you. But before you can achieve or establish this union between you and your subconscious, for it to be on a high alert level to receive from supreme power, you must be in a fully relaxed state of mind-because it doesn't need to respond to external stimuli at this point.

Always remember this is your life not mine nor anyone else but yours. Contacts to knowledge, information and willingness to indulge in all the practices that will link you to the road of your financial world is what we're talking about. So is of important that you start living your live as it pleases you not as it pleases others. Like one man rightly said, I don't have formula to success to give you, but I can give you formula to failure which is keep listening to everyone and keep working all your energy out just to please everyone. Your goal should make sense to you, and you shouldn't worry about others judging them, your major concern should be on how to achieve your desired goals that is your own purpose. Don't try to make the masses your friends, always be cautious of their influence.

The mentality of followed the crowd instead of your own intuition and instinct is not only dangerous to others but to your own character. Following crowd can lead you to losing control of yourself including your path in life. Mingling and associating with people in the society is not a bad idea, but since we are determined to discipline ourselves based on that which we want to accomplish, we have to at all time avoid indulging in any excesses as well as to avoid becoming too involved in group thinking and gossiping. Perhaps you will be cajoled, made fun of, or otherwise judged-peer pressured by those who want to bring you to their level.

Most at times we allowed ourselves to be troubled by the things out there, and that is one of those flaws, and for you to ascertain a total control of your mind you need to lessen the negative impact of the external factors that affect your happiness and your whole being. You must understand that you cannot avoid being troubled since you're on earth, because is inevitable. Still you have the right to chose how you respond to them, with the believe that you will overcome those troubles as time goes by-all these feelings are in you. Avoid comparing yourself with others, including anyone that is pushing you into doing that-because that person will only end up pushing you into desperate mood. Comparison is fruitless, waste of time, energy and also resources.

Looking at your progress development and learning to determine what has improved and what areas still need improvement usually involves comparing a "before" situation with a current situation. While you examine your past and your flaws in order to make future decision, you should endeavor to live in the present as much as possible. For example, in Buddhism, the law of here and now (law of karma) is connected to ideas about accepting the truth of your reality. The Buddhist equally link this karma to the theme of truly living in the present moment.

For you to be mentally and physically balance you need to stand with your two foots-clinging too hard to the past feelings, experiences, belief and what people did or said about you, will make you have one of your foot in the past and that will affect your current stay. The law of Here and Now is reminding us that the present is all we really have and that it is there to be fully engaged with and enjoyed. Your happiness and judgment should be based on behavior, rather than words or external sources. Knowing that we can't control and cannot rely on external events only ourselves and our responses guarantees our happiness and joy.

The only real estate you actually control in life is your mind. Take your standard news story about a tornado devastating a town, or record flooding. What does it show? Just how exposed we are to the whims of nature. All that money, time, and energy people put into their homes their businesses all of it destroyed in a fraction of a second. It's morbid and terrifying to think about, I just want you to see that nothing on earth worth taking your joy and your sense of self control away from you. According to Tony Robbins he said "take control of your consistent emotions and begin to consciously and deliberately reshape your daily experience of life".

Studies shows that neuroscientist have discovered that repetitive thoughts form neural pathways as neurons that fire together get wired together. That is to say, the more a particular thought or belief is activated and reinforced, the stronger these neural pathway become and the more automatically they become our go to pattern of perceiving. You may be tempted to ask what is neuro pathway and what has it got to do with mind control that we are discussing? A lot, neural pathway is the connection formed by axons that project from neurons to make synapses onto neurons in another location, to enable a signal to be sent from one region of the nervous system to another.

Your brain is the master organ of your body, is assigned with multitude of vital brain functions that are regulated and accomplished quite efficiently-but for the purpose of which this book is designed, we will channel our focus on the thinking and reasoning aspect, which also are parts of the functions and responsibilities of the brain. This discovery and definition was made available for you to see that you possess the power of initiating a new progressive concept of idea for your personal growth, power to think and reason because you are what you think. And by thinking you are forming a new neural pathway that in turn will change your life experiences for better.

Now thinking and reasoning is performed by the frontal lobe of the cerebral cortex. And this is what distinguishes you or makes you an advanced creature over all creatures on the universe. Your cognition or that intellect capacity in you as a human is the weapon that enables you to fight your way out of that situation-and verify some fact about it. That is why it is very important that you know, that is undiluted fact that development of knowledge, in that area or in that place that you wish to see yourself tomorrow is solely due to the marvelous potential of your brain work-through thinking and reasoning. That is why even your physical moves is typically initiated and coordinated in your brain that makes it the master organ that controls the whole body.

But at the very root of the thinking, there is a very simple-though not an easy way of living but it pays in the end. Taking absolute control of your life start immediately you start controlling what goes on in your mind. And to do that you have to at all cost, turn that which you view now as an obstacles in your life into your advantage. Control what you can and accept what you cannot is the point. According to modern day philosopher and writer Nassim Nicholas Taleb he says "transform your fear into prudence, your pain into information, mistake into initiation and desire into understanding". You have every opportunity to be a powerful creator of your own consciousness or to be passive heirs to the autopilot programming of your own history and external authorities.

When you are operating unconsciously on autopilot you are selectively perceiving an experience by interpreting them in a way that is in aligning with your existing goals, dreams, purpose, mission, passion, believe, hopes and so on. Only the thought that are conveyed with genuine emotions makes it to the back of your mind and only the thoughts that are backed up by a strong emotion stay there. Unfortunately, the negative emotions are usually stronger than the positive ones. It's important you eliminate every negative thought emotion loaded in you, what is it that happened and identify itself as bad or good? All these impression is in us of good or bad.

Our mood is ever stable, is us that turn on the mood into good or bad. Because in reality, we process what happens to us and label them good or bad and this is what leads to happiness or unhappy mood. For example, two may found themselves in a terrible situation one may think that is disastrous and get depressed. While the other person may look upon it as an opportunity to move to a better path of life. That is to say, our happiness depends on how we react to that happens to us. What exactly do you want out of life? But before you react to that question, I want you to understand one thing and that thing is the role of money on earth. Because the issue of money is the fastest thing that influence the mind very quickly-so for you to control this, you need to know and make it clear the role of money on earth and of cause in your life.

You're not existing because of money that is one fact you need to know, rather you're existing to innovate and explore your environment with GOD given latent or talent. While money is in existence because of you-to serve you as a tool for accomplishment of those goals in your mind. Things start going on negatively the moment you start or join the crowd with their general conception towards man and money. Every one want money but only few really knows what to do with it. A lot of people have mixed up the purpose of man and the purpose of money on earth, and this is part if not the main reason why things are turning upside down in the life of many. People turning themselves into slave for money, because that is what they have long trained their subconscious mind to believe. And for the fact that subconscious is there to receive command irrespective of the nature of the order (good or bad) it brings out to you what you deposited.

That is why the reflection of this repeated thought in the mind of these two classes of people in our world today (the poor believes that they were born to work and die for money, while the rich believes money were made to work for them) keep responding according to our believes. Seventy to Eighty percent of people I interviewed, to know their view over what they desire most in life said is money. I personally has no problem with their view over money, my only concern is that we should be more rational in reasoning when it comes to the issue of money to avoid misconception. Because money I know is just a mere paper and numbers that are traded for a person's time and effort.

Money is not a vision, passion, nor a goal. You just have to stop thinking in the same direction with the poor when it comes to money-because when you do, you are only making yourself vulnerable to be used by some greedy folks out there to achieve their aim. And this will automatically hamper your freedom of liberty, freedom of self-expression, freedom of time to explore in your natural potentials, you will lose control of your own life style only to be controlled by external. And that is a product and reward of your mental believe and exercise all this years. When your virtue of integrity, honor, and prestige is indirectly seized because of money, then what are you?

I know this is not the kind of life you dream for yourself but unfortunately you found yourself on it, which some time affect the way you reason and think about yourself, you saw also the decrease in your will power for taking charge of your thought. But not too worry you are not alone. Is never too late for mind rebuilding, all you have to do is to start having a re-think very fast. You have to replace "I want money" with "I need an idea". This idea is what will create wealth and that will change your entire life and that of your unborn generations. Stop taking that risk of training your mind with inferiorities rather fill and convince yourself that money was made for growth and development of mankind not the other way round. You can't sincerely read and digest all the information's with diligent practice both physical and mental exercises in this book and still remain a servant to money, is not possible.

I experienced it and that is why I share it with you. Money truly was made to serve man not man serving money. For you to get hold of your mind and gain that total chain of control that you desire you need to master yourself and mastering yourself is mastering your emotions, here are what you need to know. There is three forces that control your emotions, the emotional triad- your physiology, your language and your focus. And for you to control your mind effectively and be in charge of yourself you must know how your feelings and your body are interconnected.

Your feelings are dictated by your movement. How you use your body affects how you feel mentally and emotionally. According to Tony Robbins he says "where focus goes, energy flows", that is to say where you put your focus on is where you set your intention. Focusing on what matters to you and what you are working to achieve is the secret to success and that automatically makes you autonomy over your mind and total control of your life. Paying attention to things that holds you back is a disaster, that is why you have to be at alert to what you think, what you speak, and what you do all these are forming you gradually.

But in all this remember the judgment of others do not matter as much as your own, you must strive to live with virtue and integrity, because at the end of the day it is yourself, ourselves we must face. Try and reduce stress through exercise your mind and your body are deeply connected, the mind can make the body stressed, and physical stress in the body can lead the mind to feel stressed. Therefore it is important to reduce stress to conserve mind-control. Getting some exercise will help you to relax and breathing in deeply and holding your breath for a few seconds then slowly exhaling over the course of several seconds will also help you to center your focus.

The truth is that the world we are living in today, is hard and difficult for the poor and the average people in our society to cover their day to day expenses, with the average salaries they receive on a monthly basis. This also affect the way we think which arouse the quest for more, but is the more forth coming? If you are not satisfied with what is in your hand now, how sure are you that you will be satisfy with the more? Asking for more to me is like "tomorrow" that has no end on the surface of the earth. Same as your desire for more salary, for human desire has no end.

Until you initiate an idea that will be attracting money for you and make you less consumer of other people's product (which is actually a result of their own thought and idea) you will always ask for more. While we can't deny our physical reality, we can always make conscious efforts to change our mindset from negative to positive. Such transition is more effective through meditation. This is an act of meditating and focusing your mind on a particular thought or activity to train attention and awareness.

You need to get rid of limiting believes and open yourself to the concept of meditation for the manifestation of your desired aim and goals. This will help you keep your dreams and your aspirations alive and fresh in your mind. Remember your mind is copying all this exercises, is also processing the outcome which is the result. You need to take it serious. Meditation is something you can do anywhere you find yourself most especially when you are alone and free from external distraction. Your conscious is waiting to take your order and your subconscious mind is ever ready to receive any thing you send as a message.

But when there is no order or any task to work on, that is when your mind will start jumping from one thought to another wasting the time you should have used for creativity. You need to engage your mind in something every day. For example, remember those days in school, during exam if for instance the whole questions to attempt during exam is five in number, and you intend to start from number 1, but the answer is not forth coming immediately due to time you leave it to solve other ones to come back to it later, if you have experienced before you finish attempting the rest of the questions you see the answer of that number 1, popping in from nowhere, and I tell you that is your subconscious at work.

Communicating with yourself is another force which you must imbibe in your mind, you shouldn't over-look it the way you talk to yourself internally and out loud determines how you operate in the world. You need to change some words like "why is this things happening to me?" to "what can I do to better this situation that are already here?" when you ask why, you are not accepting the challenge and when you are not accepting the challenge you are missing the lesson that came with it in disguise. Every situation came to you for a reason and that reason is that lesson you need to figure out for growth.

If you become upset or furious over it you become emotional depressed and powerless, and when all this happens you totally lose control of yourself. Self-Improvement start from the minute you recognize your own flaws. Not one of us is perfect, and identifying which areas of yourself need to work on is crucial if you don't see the problems how can you find the solutions? If you really want to be in control of your mind you have to be a realist accepting what is, and for solution. And to maintain your state of peace and harmony which is the secret of happiness you have to live in accordance with the universal reason that is the happiest way to live.

You don't question the plans of the universe. We start facing problem and worry from the moment we allow our passions and emotions to influence our decision, and when this happens, we won't be able to find happiness nor have access to control our mind. You must try not to let yourself to be controlled by pleasure or pain. Always remember that every mental exercises has consequences if we don't control them. That is why you need to be mindful of what you say, think and do make sure you stay positive all the time. And always remain focus fix your eyes on the future, not on the past, nor present. If you must think back let it be for assessment purpose only.

Information is power when you are able to understand the fact that you are the master of your own thought, including the three forces of emotional triad psychology, you will be able to use them to your advantage and ultimately be a master of your emotions. Everything we do, think, or deeds positive or negative, good or bad, create a corresponding energy that comes back to us in some form or another. For example "the Law of Cause and Effect", is one of the laws of karma which tells us that in order to get the things we want, we must also embody those things, this simply means that whatever you sacrifice your energy doing, thinking, talking daily is the result you will receive in return whether good or bad.

ACTION

The path to success is to take massive, determined action.

Tony Robbins

Being filled with the fruits and the secret of breaking the chain of lack and want, slavery, indecisiveness and pay-cheque, into unlimited flow of income in your life and in the life of people around you, are feelings still held by few. They're serious and fury they possess the will power to take practical action to deal and make the obstacle become the only way. They understand with every clarity that the impediment to action advances action, that whatever stands in the way becomes the way to that desired dream goal-which must reflect on the outside as an evidence of their believe.

Remember faith without work is dead, but it becomes alive and manifested in your life when you put it into practice. Allow the force of your earnest expectation and hope for victory build your boldness and encourage you to act so that the source of your breath (GOD) will be magnified and HE will be proud of you. If you really want to escape the things that harass you, what you need is not to be in different place but to be a different person. Make sure that your daily routine depict exactly the picture you have in mind concerning your destiny.

Don't let inaction kill your motivation and dreams rather act instead-for lion never cowardice in the face of his prey. Press yourself so hard (don't worry you will not die) to be between your challenge and victory-this will only result to one thing which is a strong feeling and desire to depart to be where you want to be-and that is the only place that will give you peace of mind and happiness. Your flesh will feel the pain but you have to be confident in your believe, believe in yourself-with a strong affirmation like "I know my victory is close I can feel it" saying this repeatedly morning, noon and night before bed-with thanks giving to your creator in prayer for wishes fulfilled in advance will smooth the process of your request.

You will see yourself being refreshed and happy. If you can't give any account of what happened while you're deep asleep till the time you wake-up this morning, then is a enough reason for you to believe that, that mysterious power that is behind your sleep and still wake you up every day without you knowing anything about it is watching and He is able. Is waiting for you to take a step of action that will change your destiny and is obvious if not you is no one else. And the only way to solidify your faith and prove your loyalty, is by giving credit upon this Supreme force and HIS authority-which is based on furnished evidence. That is your duty here and I don't think is difficult-for anyone to do. Let your conduct anywhere you find yourself on earth be worthy of your request.

Behave and act in line with your thanks giving as one who has received. Don't miss the sight of your motivation-if you do, you will lose the urge and when there is no urge nothing works. Act in one spirit avoid division of emotion (doubt whether your desire will manifest or not), doubt will yield you no fruit and it will affect your action and effectiveness. I want to believe that by now we have graduated from being terrified over your adversity for it is clear to you now that, those things are there but not to kill you nor to harm or stay forever, but to let you see the need for you to migrate from where you are now to another level. That is to say you are the only person who has the right to make that situation permanent.

The reason you learn, study sacrifice your time in acquiring knowledge is not for decoration sake, but because you want growth in your life and for that growth to occur you have to work it out yourself. Action is an act that occurs as a result of your thought and feelings. That is why is only through this act that thought could be published on the surface of the earth. Therefore, you need to delete the spirit of hurry and download in you the spirit of patience. Succinctly, one of the laws of Karma, the Law of Patience and Reward claims that all of your greatest successes require consistent hard work.

If you're in a hurry to make it, you will find yourself in a state of desperation which normally goes with you accepting anything on the way good or bad leaving you with no options to evaluate. And this kind of move always returns back with regret and ultimate disappointment. Your success will be minor in comparison to what you're capable of achieving in life. Instead, believe that everything is in progress and is working out for your good while you keep on the little work in your hand at the moment.

When you perform your mental exercise without accompanying it with physical effort which is your action your expected result will not complete. When you subject yourself to think over a particular thing for at least one hour each day consistently without breaking it doesn't matter whether is your first time of thinking about it or not what you're simply doing is that you are initiating and creating a supernatural force that will bring your thought into reality. You don't think based on your current status, think in connection with that Super force that takes you to bed at night and brings you back in the morning.

That is too mysterious for your carnal knowledge to comprehend. This Supreme force is the source and the controller of all the activities of the universe. Total submission to your mental exercise, and total submission to this thought will make your believe very stronger and you will begin to see that truly, thoughts are indeed things. When you become faithful to this hour(s) including sincerely indulgence to other exercises, first thing you will begin to notice is this, your thoughts will gradually start influencing your physical steps towards achieving that which you have been sacrificing your time thinking and doing every day.

If you are a beginner to this mental exercise-of course you know that is where everything start from, then you have to beware of break in transmission because it will lead to another and immediately this fatigue set in, you're already disassociating and disconnecting the neuron pathways that are already into forming process for your progress. Achieving your goals takes repeated action and you can't give up too early. High self-esteem can give you the drive, determination, and personal power necessary to take these actions and be persistent until you achieve success.

You can't afford to go back after coming this far or to start from the scratch do you? May be you don't know, you are a product of a Super natural force, with a name for easy identification in the universe, that is why your person can never been found anywhere in the world. And if a manufacturer is not proud of his product he won't be proud enough to give it a name, the reason why he gave his product a name is for the consumers to know and identify his product. And how good the product is determines the level of praise the producer will get in return, you are just a product of this Super force that governs the universe, imagine how proud HE will be seeing you shine-immediately you let that star in you out, people will bow to HIS Might Authority because you belong to HIM.

You are like a loaded gun and the observers are waiting to hear the sound of your bullet. If you find yourself in the midst of losers am sorry-for you may not be able to act as you should as a spirited winner. The only thin line which I know that separate winners and losers are their thinking and action that means the way the both behave. Taking action means stepping forward and show casing the very best of yourself. Your action speaks for you wherever you go in life. For you to get equal reaction (reward or result) you have to apply equal force that means physical force that is equivalent to what you are thinking to do. For example, if you are thinking of passing your exams with good grade, then you must be ready to bend down and sacrifice your hours in reading before you can accomplish that thought.

The best way to invoke the spirit of activeness into achieving that goals is to keep yourself on a serious check, bombarding yourself with questions like, what do I really want my life to look like in weeks, months or years to come? Will this my current routine of life get me there? This will make you get serious in setting up your goals and that should be part of your life's journey it should be relevant and meaningful to you. When you set up your goals it will give you a sense of focus and direction of action on what to be doing each time of the day. It will show you clearly the areas that need to be develop in your life.

You have heard, I mean is no more a new news that writing down your goals on a paper is the starting point of achieving any meaningful thing in life. When I read about writing down your goals on a paper read it morning and before bed, I never knew that behind every instruction been given from people who have made it-lies a great wisdom and power, because that instruction came out of their experience. So I didn't take it serious to be honest for the first time I read it from the book titled "Think and Grow rich" by Napoleon Hill, but as I continued with my reading habit-I kept on seeing and hearing the same thing from different books and motivational speakers, that is when I said no, this must be a prerequisite to what I am looking for in life so I decided to apply this technique to know how it will work.

Here is what I started experiencing, before I step out of my house I look at the piece of paper where I wrote goals and things that I need to accomplish for the day, that piece of paper became my road map each day I woke up, it changed my daily routine to a routine that is pointing at those direction that I wished to go in life, that is my path. But note, before you lay a foundation success you must have putting many factors into consideration before arriving at conclusion of determination some of the factors are, not everyone will be ok with your new choice, some will desert you for it, you will be criticized as a result of your decision.

It is very obvious that when you don't plan or organize your day you will be confuse on what to do or think at every given time. That was exactly how my life was very disorganized but immediately I indulge in following my stated goals and to-do-list, my life did not only get shape, but as time goes by I began to notice that those goals of mine are now sticking to mind. Though it wasn't an easy way and I wasn't expecting it to be easy either, getting yourself down and fix your attention into work is the price and that is the only direction to a successful end. When you start working with your to-do-list it normally invoke a kind of force, forcing you to do that which you have mapped out to do even when the flesh is weak.

Study shows that you have 45 percent more likely to achieve your goals if you write them down. After writing your goals down, come up with an action plan and make sure you follow it up actively "action" they say speaks louder that voice. Swim into action don't wait for anybody to push you, you have to push yourself to do it. Make sure you don't confuse yourself with multiple task, break your goals into smaller parts, set them according to your priorities, don't try to accomplish all in one day is a step by step. And be specific.

When you break your goals into smaller parts, give yourself a mandate-this means setting a deadlines this will channel all your mind and attention in making sure that, the date which you marked to accomplish that particular goal you meet it. This will motivate you to move forward to the next goal on the list. Everything big starts on a very small note, from there it will escalate beyond your imagination. Warren Buffet one of the richest men in the universe today started building his wealth and other things he controls today from doing petty business celling magazine from door to door.

You mustn't wait to mark it big before you start acting on your dreams and it doesn't matter where you're standing right now-because that particular time in your mind, that time you are sitting down waiting for, before you take action will never come is an illusion believe me. Get this clear and fix it into your head, the best time to act is now. As you know time waits for no one. That vision that goal that dream remains in your mind, and it will remain there until you pull them out. And remember, that day you were born, a date for your departure on earth were also born, but very unfortunate no one knows the date of his/her own demise, that is why the spirited winner work on "Now"

Logically, between the date of your birth and the date of your death is now, and is a big privilege for you. So what you do today is what will be attached to your life history or biography when you leave the world of mortal, and that is what your generation will remember you for. I don't want you to waste a single minutes any more, I don't want you to live your life as if is permanent-of course is not, as the time is ticking so our expiration date on earth is fast approaching. Is a reality and is a fact and it makes no sense if we shy away from it because is something is and will continue to be.

If you observe, you will notice miss-comfort and miserable on the faces of some people stuck-up in anger and pain even at their job, a sign that all is not well. Still many believe there's nothing they can do to change the situation and unfortunately that believe kept and will continue keeping the subscribers in bondage as a slave. Until the mind is reset including the believe, with those self-questioning you won't be able to know whether you dived into a programmed or un-programmed life of another. But if you're living a programmed live and you are not happy with what you do, you are waiting for someone to make you smile the smile you owe yourself, then you may be on a wrong page in the book of life.

Is someone somewhere happy while you go angry and sad? Did you exchange unknowingly your happiness with someone else sadness? According to Martin Luther King Jr., we all are fighting for something, trying to make change in our lives. Are you going to bend and give up? Are you going to let live ride you or are you going to refuse to roll over?

Because no amount of books will change or influence your mind if you did not develop that iron backbone with that strength of conviction and sense of duty and purpose that make it impossible to do anything but stand up. Until this power is developed in you, regardless of how entrenched or over whelming your enemies are you can never change anything in your life. In anything you do in life always remember that you have one and only life to give for your life, family, community, state, country and the world at large. So do everything you could to make it lively because you never can tell when it will cease.

If you're still asleep I want you to wake-up and open your eyes wide open this is 2020 movement, you have to deny yourself any set-back and move forward and play the game of life and for you to win you need to play your card well, don't be afraid in running this race that you have already won. Refuse to be an old lion for is only an old lion that perish for lack of prey. Don't be afraid to fail, because failure and success has a connection. You must in one way or the other experience failure before you succeed, but that doesn't mean you should judge your success with your experience.

In pursuit of wealth and becoming successful you must be wise, and we learn wisdom from failure much more than from success. We often discover what will do, by finding out what will not do; and probably he who never made a mistake never made a discovery says Samuel Smiles. For you must fail before you win is natural I can't change it and you can't either is been there is a universal order and law which every achievers in the past followed and obeyed and every intended winners must follow pass through it. Yours won't be exceptional. Many people don't take action to improve their lives after reading fine books, not because the book is not ok or interesting, no, the simple truth is that they focused more on not failing instead of aiming at succeeding.

The nature of your state of concentration will determine the first phase of your reaction. According to Taleb Hassim he says, "For life to be really fun, what you fear should line-up with what you desire". Your burning desire of what you want to achieve in life will direct your steps, actions, your relationship to people around you and the way you talk. When Washington wrote to a pre-turn coat Benedict Arnold that "it is not in the power of any man to command success, but you have done more you deserved it", fear to act on our dream can only enter the mind with our consent, Cato had been taught choose not to be afraid, and fear simply vanishes. Great people know that the road is tough but is through that toughness champion will emerge.

You can never find fulfillment in a place you are not meant to be, is not possible. You can only find fulfillment when you're in your own path and is only your action that can take you there. To be brave is to be alive and to live your dream in such a way that the world knows about it-that makes you a star, that brings out your name very well, and that makes your life meaningful. Don't allow time to surprise you. Sir Walter Raleign, writing later in Queen Elizabeth's life, saw this happening. He saw the Queen getting older and her options disappearing, as she grew older and grey. She was, he said "a lady whom time has surprised". Don't let this phrase to describe you because it describes so many people.

Is better you act now you have your life, your full energy and whatever it take to make that change. Don't let fear and procrastination make you feel you will live forever. You have to remember what Seneca said each time you want to entertain fear Seneca told us that, old age and death aren't this thing that lies off in the distant future. It's a process that's happening to us always and everywhere. Don't let time to surprise you act now or never. Without a track record of constant progress to remind you of where you're going, fear and doubt can stall you out.

Don't let inaction kill your motivation—take action instead. Wake up with a clear, defined purpose and tackle all the things that will bring you closer to your goals. The ability to concentrate on something in your environment and direct mental effort toward it is critical for learning new things, achieving goals and performing well across a wide variety of situations. Your ability to focus can mean the difference between success and failure. Focus is a lot like a mental muscle. The more you work on building it up, the stronger it gets.

Stabilizing your mental focus is not magical but a process, it takes time because you are not use to it before, and if it was simple, then we would all have the razor-sharp concentration of an elite athlete. For you to accomplish this mental focus, some changes need to be made in your daily habits. Step one you need to assess yourself mentally, within the 24 hours of the day what occupies your thoughts? How much do you concentrate on those goals? Those area you gave more attention to are what dominate and control your life and from those area comes your physical reactions.

That is exactly what has been happening, sometimes you see yourself doing things you don't really or like to do and those ones you love and wish to do you don't do it. You feel happy and excited giving thought to that wonderful idea that you know will change your life if automatically implemented, suddenly the bunch of already stored routine now stormed in the process of this meditation and steal the focus away leaving you with no option, other than as usual result as a result of the old pattern of life. Because when you do the same thing every day you will keep getting the same result. Until you discover yourself, until you know who you are, until you know how important it is to create your own path you can never be fulfilled in life.

For you to be free from the bondage of lack and want which many people are experience and still experiencing with eagerness and zeal to evacuate, you have to create and shape your own flow. And most importantly, please do everything humanly possible to avoid leaving your fate of survival, your children and your unborn generation in the hand of someone, no matter who that person is to you, is dangerous, you will only leave your blood on the middle of the road to continue the hard where you stopped-that is if they survive the danger of standing in the middle of busy road. According to Robert Green in one of his books titled 48 Laws of Power, he instructed us on the Law no. 2: Never put too much trust in friends. But I tell you never put too much trust in human folks (in general).

For you to start seeing different result as a result of the new life you're craving for, you need to start the process of initiating a new positive thought with an act that will channel you into it. Fear not about "how" for what is in you is able just make yourself available. Before then you have to understand one fact, you have to pull the energy first, that energy and the force behind it will attract that which is beyond your imagination that some time tempt you to ask "How". I can only show you the way to your financial well is left for you to explore.

To be mentally strong to conquer your world of financial lack, you need to stay alert at all time to monitor whatever that comes to your mind, but how can you stay alert when we are surrounded with constant distractions. Like mails, social media if you are not on WhatsApp, you are on Facebook, Instagram and so on and so forth. You can never control any of this distractions if you don't observe your rules and time as a person. People that create all those things it took them time, energy, focus, meditation, effort, resources and so on, to bring thought into creation.

All these sectors are good don't get me strong, but I want you to ask yourself this beautiful question, do you think if those inventors of most of the things that take much of our time today wasn't dedicated and committed to what they were doing do you think they would have succeeded in creating something like Facebook, TV, WhatsApp, Tencent QQ, Instagram, Twitter, Skype, Viber etc. they wouldn't have. I think they are more prudent in whatever they are doing including the way they spend their time, for the sake of the course they were pursuing. Rebuilding yourself for success you need to regulate and control how you spend your time.

If you exhaust all your time, resource and energy on all those things, how much is left for your own self recreation? The time you wasted today can never return back to you again believe me, you may lost money today, and gain it tomorrow. But time wasted is completely lost, the only way out to regain your wasted time is by making it up to yourself with future time and that future is now. What am trying to let you know here is very simple, don't be programmed with or allowed yourself to be programmed by people's events, you have to design your own time and give yourself a mandate to follow up whatever you mapped out to do in connection to your goals and vision.

Staying on task is very difficult, but when you break your goals into smaller parts and you are taking it one at a time, occupying your time with each one of them consistently and regularly without breaking the routine, will make your distractions to fade away. You must be at alert don't lose track on this process for progress to emerge. Make sure your mentality towards achieving success is stabilize. If you don't stabilize your own mentality towards achieving your own greatness those pretenders in your life who haven't helped themselves will get you confuse with a camouflage face.

Be careful of them they celebrate your frowning face in secret and your sad mood as you waste your precious time trading on their own path every day and night. Pause for a while, ask yourself what will be the fate of my unborn generation if I continue like this without any effort to make change? I think is far better to trade on your own path than to keep trading on another path created by someone else. Don't live a life as if you are not going to leave the universe someday, make your own mark before you leave the world of the mortal for immortal.

The world is waiting, I myself is also waiting to see your rainbow in the sky. You can never ever make a move of action unless you make failure your friend, until you make up your mind and ready to ignore people with their saying it will be hard for you to take serious action in developing yourself. Great achievers don't care or listen to what people say, because they always have something to say about someone and that is part of their job, but winners don't care and they pay more attention to themselves and act based on what they believe is good and truth for themselves not lies that are coming from mediocrities.

And that is why there is and will continue to be a big gap between the rich and the poor. The reason why you shouldn't listen to that lie people say about you is because is invalid, secondly is baseless when it comes to your dreams, vision, aspirations and your mission on earth which is strictly known by you and your GOD alone. So why should you believe people's judgement over your life? If you are still doubting whether what people are saying about you is right or wrong try moving to another environment you will still observe different opinion and different point of view from people over you. So what?

This is the main reason why you should disassociate and disconnect yourself from how minded people because they will only bring you to their low class of thinking and believe. Listen to that your inner voice and work to discover who you are and for you to do this correctly and accurately you need to access your past, present and the future that is where you are heading to. I always ask myself what it will profit me if I stay and sacrifice my whole life living another man's dream.

How much time will be left for me to initiate and develop mine own dreams? And for me to escape this miserable life in future I have to act now that I have the strength and energy because the more you grow the more your energy is exhausting. See is only when you engage yourself in a critical thinking (not negative but positive) you will begin to get revelation about what you don't know before about yourself. Our brain is always active to work but sometimes it need to be activated.

Our brain is like a baby that supposed to go to school but still lying down in the bed, is your duty as a mother or father to this child to wake him up and get him ready for school, but if you don't the kid will relax and enjoying the sleep. This scenario is no different from the way our brain operate when you don't think of anything useful for yourself the mind will go wild sometimes out of control. If you don't face your brain with unusual questioning it will not do anything, it will just be there. Is like when you have AK 47 rifle and a person with mere knife is challenging you for a fight. The only way the person with a knife can win is when you're ignorance of what you are holding.

You need to harness into your brain box very well to join the lively group of this world. When you lack liberty, freedom, happiness, joy, when you are living in misery are you lively? This live is full of opportunity and is a big privilege that you are alive today that means HE who gave you breath is not yet done with you. Many have gone great beyond while many are still struggling to live. So how will you explain the fact that you lived for years without a sign, what is that "but", holding you to act? I know what I felt, I was furious I was hungry to see my goals in life standing right before me.

The furiousness of achieving success got deeper in me, to the extent that I became mad at myself each time I allowed one hour pass by without being properly fixed into something that will change the situation as at then for better. And to GOD I re-turn all the glory my self-discipline and the hard training I imposed on myself including the one nature imposed on me, and my acceptance and total commitment and dedication to change mine then situation, those actions I took then saw me where I am today.

Life of a slavery is very terrible, is very bad, is horror, is hot, he who has never experience fire burn will never understand the pain. I don't wish you that experience or the life of a slavery either. But if you are not fulfilled in life, if you're always mad at yourself, with what you do, there may be little or no different between you and the way a slave feels because both of you almost lacks the same thing happiness, freedom, restrictions in one way or the other in some of your ways in life. The logic is very simple, if you are not fulfilled if you are not comfortable with where you found yourself right now, if you are always having emotional depression each time your alarm wakes you up on a Monday morning for work, analyzes the characteristic of a slave to see if you could find a different.

Is only action that will push you out in living a life of your dream. You are required to change your thought of negativity to positivity for a positive result and reward that is if you're still dowelling in negative emotion. Live your dream never you think of quitting because it won't help anybody it will make you a loser and a fool in the end. For you to be totally free and happy you need to first acknowledge the fact that you are not on your path and that is affecting your joy and happiness you can't be on your call and still you remain unhappy. Secondly accept the challenge (i.e. the pain, the restrictions, the pressures, and other suffering that comes with it) knowing that is not permanent will make your mind to relax and search for nearest exit (solutions).

The world is full of people's innovations, dreams and ideas, the world are waiting to see yours too. One question you hear the comedian Marc Maron ask a lot of standups and actors at the beginning of his interviews is who did you come up with? Who were your guys? Who was there at the beginning with you? We are shaping the scene we are in just as it is shaping us. Our fate is bound up with other people and their gain is not our loss. When we are with right people, we help each other and help the world when we excel and fulfil our potential.

You must be abnormal to be normal, whenever you are creating your own path in life. New life comes from a new mind a new way of looking at yourself and your life. If you're dreaming to be where they are, if you are dreaming to acquire wealth and become great and live a life free live like great achievers does, then you have to be willing to do what they do. Champions don't just talk and learn, they learn and act on what they have leant. That is what separate them from the crowd and that is the movement of the great people. You have to be ready to be on top of the game no matter what it cost and that is the spirit. No matter how dry the jungle is a lion can never indulge in eating grass

Remember what Aurelius wrote, perhaps after one of his failures "if you accept the obstacles and work with what you're given, an alternative will present itself another piece of what you're trying to assemble". The seeker of wealth, truth, happiness, freedom and fame in any area of life will necessarily be the man who is interested in obeying the rules and regulations guiding quests. And what they must understand is that where there are rules, all cannot favor your formal way of life style. Therefore you should carry an open mind and learn to adapt and expect the unexpected as you strive for success.

However, an evolutionary unique and fascinating way of learning in humans is through instruction, we learn and grow through spoken words or books. And for the things we believe is true and learn, to have effect in us is only when we practices them. Always have it mind that everything becomes stronger when the force behind it is strong, and it becomes weaker if the force is weak. If your action towards that goal is weak and low the chance of accomplishing that goal may be far fetch. But if your action is full of force and energy let say 80 to 90 percent of your daily energy is been channeled towards achieving that goal then your success is at the corner.

Avoid desperation, the spirit of desperation indicates that you want it your own way and timing. But genuine success actually should happen in alignment with the universal and your destiny timing on earth. You don't predict or command GOD to do your will, but you can design through your thought, planning and action. This thing is a gradual process. It is necessary you equipped yourself with all this pre-information it will enable you to solidify your decision to commit everything you have got in exchange of what you believe will come.

There are always a reason to put off change, to put off getting committed and being serious, to keep going as you always have. But just because there are "reasons" doesn't mean you have an excuse. It certainly doesn't mean that subsequent years ahead of you are going to treat you with kid gloves. You have all the energy all the time on this planet to accomplish any task you wish to accomplish. The maximum the energy and time invested in that goal determines the result that you will get in return.

That is more reason why you are to start now don't wait any further for the time wasted today can never be retrieved again for live. Your time and your energy should be working together to achieve a common goal. Your thought is energy your action is energy all these are engulfed with time all is running within the cycle of the 24 hours that make up a day. Your dream should be your action. When you dream and act in opposite of your thought you did not only waste your time but energy. All this need to be carefully watched by who? By you.

This is the part of reprogramming of your system for better result (i.e. your destiny, your future, your goals, your vision all these defines your race in life). Becoming rich is a process not an event. Riches is an exchange of hard labor for wealth, you don't buy rich you make it. Is more of doing than talking, everyone can talk on how he want to become rich, but only few went ahead and do what it takes to become rich. See yourself among those that will make it in the end not just talking it. If you don't know the direction that is leading to your destiny you wouldn't know when you are there, pass or know the requirements that will take you there.

But when you know where you are going and the requirements, your journey will be smooth and it will get you prepared for the task ahead with full confident to face any challenge. Your goal settings will show your work, it will invite feedback and discuss your solution and as your mind is searching for solution and the nearest exit, ask yourself what are the requirements, what are my strengths and weaknesses, which area do I need to develop for me to become expert as soon as am out, what kind of skills do I have, those ones I lack what kind of self-help book will be ok for me?

When all these thought are going on you are exercising your mind, tasking the universe through your mind for solution and persistently and consistently doing this, your steps your thought will start having a different shape with a different direction. Remember this adage that says "when you found yourself in a thick forest you don't shout until you come out" meaning your moves towards your progress should be kept secret to yourself, until your aim is achieved. I want to believe that by now we are on the same page for success and for the sake of what you are pursuing in life you have to find it worthy to eliminate some unhealthy and unproductive activities, including firing distractions that hardly prevent you from focusing on the real thing.

The problem most people do face when they finish reading strong book like this is that they thought that this transformation is something that will happen overnight, or immediately they finish reading the book. Please note it doesn't happen that way, remember you are working to change intuitive thoughts feelings, and emotions that have been there for years and this has been the way you have been operating. So what makes you think the change will come in one night? That is why you have to put full-stop to procrastination and proceed to action.

Because the earlier you start taking action in changing your previous neuron pathways, the earlier you give birth to new neuron pathways and that will make your cerebrum to start coming together in the same page to keep you moving forward in achieving your new aim and purpose of initiating the pattern. To know that something is the way it is or work the way it does is knowledge, understanding it will push you to act for you to experience what you know and believe is true, which involve your intuitive thought, emotions and feelings. All this demand your patience for the system to adjust from the previous ways of operation to the new pattern which comes with new believe with new faith.

For your sincere fellowship in this book from the beginning until now, being confident of this very work, just as it is right for me to think of sharing this good news with you, shows that I have you in my heart and I want you to be a partaker with me and others in enjoying the grace and power that flows from this book, therefore, I hope that the prompt implementation of the recommendations of my extraordinary information on this book, will enable us collectively meet our various challenges against lack and wants in any areas of our endeavors which appears to be an obstacle to our happiness and pleasant life we ought to be living as human.

DON'T forget, is only your will to win, the desire to succeed, the urge to reach your full potential are the keys that will unlock the door to your personal excellence. If the knowledge and the information, you gathered in this book does not determine your action yet, then you missed something I suggest re-read the book for the second time, because I crave to hear your own testimony when you finally climbed the ladder of greatness.

"Happiness and freedom begin with one principle. Some things are within your control and some are not".
Epictetus-Stoic philosopher.

REFERENCE

www.verywellmind.com
www.littlethingsmatter.com
www.biblestudytools.com
www.huffpost.com
www.studybuddhism.com
www.businessdictionary.com
www.collegeinfogeek.com
www.psycom.net
www.happify.com
www.talkingcharge.csh.umn.edu
www.personaltao.com
www.wakeupcloud.com
www.philosophystackexchange.com
www.lightbearers.org
www.theodysseyonline.com
www.ncbi.nlm.nih.gov
www.inc.com
www.goodread.com
www.biography.com
My wealthshop By Frank
Think and Grow Rich by Napoleon Hill

Printed in the United States
By Bookmasters